The Manufacturer's Book *of* Lists

Compiled and Edited by Gene Marks

Quicker Better Wiser Publications
Bala Cynwyd, PA

ISBN-13: 978-1492779186
ISBN-10: 1492779180

Images © 2013

Gene's previous books include the #1 Amazon Small Business Best Seller *The Streetwise Small Book of Lists* (Adams Media), *The Small Business Desk Reference* (Alpha Books), *Outfoxing The Small Business Owner – Crafty Techniques For Creating A Profitable Relationship* (Adams Media), *The Complete Idiot's Guide to Successful Outsourcing* (Alpha Books), and *In God We Trust – Everyone Else Pays Cash* (Quicker!Better!Wiser Publications)

All articles reprinted by special permission

This publication is designed to provide accurate and authoritative information with regard to the subject matter covered. It is sold with the understanding that the author is not engaged in rendering legal, accounting, or other professional advice. If legal advice or other expert assistance is required, the services of a competent professional person should be sought.

-from a Declaration of Principles jointly adopted by a Committee of the American Bar Association and a Committee of Publishers and Associations

Acknowledgements

Thanks to the more than 60 manufacturing experts who contributed their knowledge. This book is designed to not only showcase their abilities but to provide a "yellow pages" of incredible resources for the manufacturer to draw on. Need more help? Contact them!

Thanks to Jen Deslaurier for putting this book together. Jen has become an expert in research, manuscript design and navigating the waters of publishing. Also critical to this book was Caryn Maenza who provided additional research. Lizette Maenza edited our content like a pro. And Susan Weeks' graphical design expertise has given life to our front and back covers.

My company has more than 600 clients, but the company that has had the most influence on me is Griff Paper and Film. Owned by brothers Todd, Bob, John and Alex Phinn, Griff is a leader in manufacturing specialty paper and film products and sells to thousands of customers worldwide. They have taught me much about how to run a manufacturing business. But more importantly, the Phinn brothers are an example of the kind of profitable, successful and ethical organization that every business owner in America should strive to be. Their website is www.paperandfilm.com.

Preface

You are in the manufacturing business. You are the owner. Or you are senior management. Or maybe you're middle management. And you have questions.

"What are the best ways to reduce my obsolete inventory?"

"Are there any tax credits available specifically for manufacturers?"

"What are the best metrics for measuring my plant's productivity?"

Of course there are more. You want to run your warehouse the right way. You want to find the best people and motivate them. You want to make sure you're using the right technology. These are all the issues that a manufacturer like you encounters. And of course you don't have all the answers. So you find experts. Lawyers, accountants, technology people, insurance agents, consultants, pundits. These are all people who know more than you about their specific areas of expertise. So where do you find these people?

Right here!

Here is your resource. Here is the one place with more than 70 lists from over 60 experts. Each list answers commonly asked question from a typical manufacturer. Each expert is experienced in their field. Their contact info is provided too. So feel free to reach out to them for more help.

The Manufacturer's Book of Lists is packed full of critical information that you will need to run your manufacturing business. Read it. Re-read it. And use it as a guide to making more money.

I've learned a lot about running a business over the past twenty years. But I'm no expert. These people are the experts.

Table of Contents

Chapter 1: Your Plant
10 Tips For Improving Your Warehouse Safety 10
9 Ways to Improve Your Workplace Security 13
31 Sure Ways to Lower Your Operating Assets 15
Maintenance Costs and Improve Reliability
8 Best Techniques For Forecasting Your Production 19
10 Things You Should Know About Demand Planning 21
12 Steps For Implementing a Quality Management System 25
In Your Facility
10 Performance Metrics Every Manufacturer Should Know 28
5 Ways To Measure Your Facility's Operational Excellence 32
9 Ways to Reduce Your Manufacturing Overheads 34
5 Ways To Advance Lean Manufacturing With Real-Time 37
Intelligence
10 Most Important Aspects For Managing Your Plant's 40
Manufacturing Capacity
5 Ways A Manufacturer Can Cut Energy Use 44
7 Important Zoning Law Considerations Every 45
Manufacturer Should Know

Chapter 2: Your Inventory
10 Steps for Implementing a Material Handling System 50
10 Ways Managing Inventory That Will Improve Your 54
Customer Service
20 Methods For Reducing Overstocked Inventory 57
8 Best Ways to Reduce Your Overall Inventories 59
6 Great Ways To Better Store Your Inventory 62
4 Ways To Keep Your Inventory Lean 64
7 Ideas For Turning Your Inventory Into Cash 67
8 Tips To Increase Your Inventory Turnover 69
5 Ways to Best Leverage Your "Internet of Assets" 72

Chapter 3: Your People
20 Ways That the IRS Distinguishes An Employee From A 76
Sub Contractor
6 Tactics For Avoiding Immigration Problems 80
6 Ways to Maximize Your Employee Training Dollars 82

9 Ways Outsourcing Your Manufacturing Can Improve   84
Your Business
4 Outsourcing Mistakes To Avoid   88
4 Tips And Resources For Managing Your Outsourced   91
Contracting Manufacturing Relationship
8 Most Common Federal Labor Laws Every Manufacturer   93
Should Know
12 Employee Notices You May Need To Post In Your Plant   95
10 Great Manufacturing Compensation Strategies   99
10 Rules for Determining Overtime Pay In Your Shop   102
9 Key OSHA Requirements For Your Shop   107

Chapter 4: Your Sales And Marketing

5 Interview Questions Every Manufacturer Should Ask A   112
Prospective Sales Manager
6 Things You Should Expect from a Manufacturer's Rep   115
7 Top Considerations When Hiring A Manufacturers' Rep   117
5 Ways Manufacturers Can Increase Sales   120
7 More Ways Manufacturing Companies Can Increase   123
Sales
3 Ways Manufacturers Can Use Social Media to Win   126
Business
5 Marketing Ideas Manufacturers Should Embrace and 5 to   128
Avoid
8 Marketing Tips For Manufacturers   132
7 Ways to Maximize Your Next Manufacturer's Trade   135
Show
10 Tips For Using Tradeshow Giveaways Effectively   137
10 Common Tradeshow Exhibiting Mistakes Manufacturers   140
Make
5 Reasons Manufacturers Should Offer Financing To Their   144
Customers
20 Top Tips For Doing Business In China   147

Chapter 5: Your Financials

9 Ways To Keep Your Business Overhead Under Control   152
10 More Ways For Decreasing Your Overhead   155
6 Calculations For Measuring A Manufacturer's Financial   158
Health
4 Purchasing Practices That Can Change A Manufacturer's   162
Life

11 Most Common Insurance Coverages For A Manufacturer 164

14 Things A Manufacturer Should Remember When Filing For A Patent 169

6 Places To Conduct A Trademark Search 173

10 Federal Tax Benefits Specifically For Manufacturers 175

14 Key Issues When Buying A Manufacturing Business 178

7 Financial Terms Every Manufacturer Should Know 182

4 Great Manufacturing Blogs To Follow 185

7 Things To Include In Your Break Even Analysis 187

7 Ways to Get the Most Out Of Your Financial Statements 189

10 Things Savvy Manufacturers Should Know About Crowdfunding 193

7 Reasons Every Manufacturer Needs A Business Plan 197

10 Essential Elements Of A Manufacturing Business Plan 199

5 Key Aspects For Valuing A Manufacturing Business 202

Chapter 6: Your Technology

5 Things Manufacturers Need To Know About 3D Printing 208

6 Ways Manufacturers Can Build A Profitable Digital Presence 210

6 Mobile Apps That Save Manufacturers Time And Money 212

3 Questions To Ask Your Tech Partner 214

5 Ways To Make Your Manufacturing CRM System More Productive 216

7 Questions To Ask Your Software Vendor Before You Buy 219

5 IT Project Challenges For The Typical Manufacturer 222

Chapter 1: Your Plant

10 Tips For Improving Your Warehouse Safety

Workplace safety isn't just about personal protection and the protection of your employees. We live and work in a very litigious society and the lack of a $20 safety sign can now lead to a $10,000,000 lawsuit. Based on the top 10 safety citations issued by OSHA in 2010 (in addition to the laws of common sense,) here are 10 tips that can help you to keep yourself, and your job, safe.

1. Scaffolding/Fall protection - #1 & #2 highest ranked for citations issued in 2010 with 15,864. Scaffold planking or support giving way, slipping, or being struck by a falling object were the biggest culprits here. Employees must be provided the proper fall protection at 4' in general industry, 5' in maritime environments, and 6' in construction settings. Incidentally, these two violations were ranked #1 and #2 in 2009 also.

2. Hazard tags – Material Safety Data Sheets. Learn them, live them, love them. Pay attention to them as an employee and post them as an employer and they can and will save your life. Also, always keep spill containment kits, wash stations and showers close by.

3. Respiratory Protection – Personal Protection Equipment (PPE) is required to be provided by companies whose products or manufacturing processes are hazardous to the health of the employee. It is not just up to the company to provide them however, it's also up to the employee to use them.

4. Ladder falls – Moving up two spots since 2009 with over 3,000 violations, falls from ladders are perhaps one of the most avoidable accidents that exist. Simply take the extra 10% of time that it takes to make the climb correctly, at the correct angle, and with the proper footing for the ladder. Make sure the ladder isn't falling apart, shaky, or leaning to one side and the next, and if you find yourself pausing to guess if you can make the climb, it probably isn't worth the try. Find another way.

5. Lockout/Tagout – Again, take the time to make everybody aware of the problem by tagging out or locking out the machinery or equipment that is malfunctioning. Most people would think that this is pretty self explanatory, but it bears noting that there were over 3,000 violations last year nationwide.

6. Electrical wiring/design – Please don't do this yourself unless you are a professionally certified electrician. We can all save the "weekend warrior" jobs for the house. Shortcuts may save money in the short term, but you're one mistake away from possibly putting the company out of business by lawsuit, fire, or worse (and you may be one misplaced screwdriver away from not seeing the kids graduate from high school.) Don't take the chance.

7. Guarding against floor or wall openings, holes, or hazards – Guard rail, safety nets, harnesses, floor striping, hand rails. These are all ways to avoid free falls in the workplace. And if you're the employee (or boss for that matter,) ask yourself, "Is climbing up the rack a good idea?" Use your head to think, not to break your fall.

The above constituted the top 10 citations issued by OSHA (some were combined) and the other tips below are here for additional information:

8. Exits and signage – Having enough emergency exits to evacuate the building sounds like simple logic, but I'm in

Chicago. There are plenty of buildings that were constructed decades ago and while you may have been told that the building is "grandfathered" in with regards to codes, lawsuits don't care about that. Even if you win, you're still paying a lawyer. Check with your OSHA rep. If all that is needed are signs, spend the $100 or so.

9. Head/eye protection – We all know that 99% of the time, nothing happens that requires the dire or immediate need for protection. Everybody has to remember that you're not protecting yourself against the 99%, but the 1%. Wear the gear, and if you don't like what it does to your hair (yes, I've heard that reason before,) then go work in the office.

10. Clean workspace – Pallet shards or oil spills on the floor, blowing then melting snow on the dock, or anything else that might seem small has the potential to turn into a ten-million dollar problem. Take the extra couple of minutes and keep it clean because a dirty workplace can actually contribute (or exacerbate) any of the other nine concerns outlined above.

These are just ten general hints, and there are plenty more depending upon your individual operation. For additional OSHA regulation, citation, or violation information, see the OSHA website or contact your OSHA representative.

Jeremy Shaw is the Co-Owner and Operating Manager of the American Material Handling Equipment Company of Illinois, LLC (amhec.com). He is a seasoned and principled business professional experienced in small business operations, sales management, and customer service and retention. With knowledge and skill cultivated from nearly a decade in the industrial sector as a material handling equipment consultant, he is also educated in the telecommunications, trade show exhibit construction, and hospitality industries.

9 Ways To Improve Your Workplace Security

Opportunistic thieves consider office buildings as easy targets. Even a workmate could be a potential thief. Workplace violence is the most important security threat to America's largest corporations, followed closely by crisis management. the workplace security concerns are common in every part of the world, even in Australia where our expert is.

1. Lock it up or lose it - Thieves usually look for items of value such as laptop computers, mobile phones and electronic equipment they can easily sell. Staff property, such as wallets and valuables, will also be stolen if not locked up.

2. Make sure you have up-to-date security - Office security needs constant attention. Thieves will always be looking for opportunities. If your building has up-to-date security measures in place and alert staff, it may deter or prevent a theft.

3. Check security procedures for all building entry and exit points - Check for any faults and weaknesses in the security procedures you use. Thieves will take advantage of any opportunities to gain undetected access, such as through faulty fire doors and elevators; unattended loading docks and unattended reception areas.

4. Encourage staff to approach unknown visitors - Thieves often gain entry to buildings by 'tailgating' a legitimate staff member. Security and other relevant staff should question people who are not wearing identification and establish if they have authority for being on the premises. a security process should be in place to deal with this sort of situation.

5. Establish an assets register - Make sure your assets register contains the make, model and serial numbers of all your office equipment and is kept in a secure area.

6. Nominate a security coordinator - It is recommended that one person in each office be nominated to be responsible for security issues. Their role should include: Regularly conducting a security audit of the office; raising security concerns at staff meetings; liaising with other tenants or offices in the building; making recommendations to improve security, and liaising with building security.

7. Install security system warning signs to deter thieves - Warning signs at entry points to the building can inform a potential thief of your security systems and deter them from entering the building. (For example, if you use 24 hour video surveillance, put up a sign advertising the fact.)

8. Network with other tenants about security issues - To have a broader understanding of the security issues that affect your office it is important that you liaise with building management and other tenants. This can be mutually advantageous.

9. Report all suspicious or criminal activity to police - If you hear something or see something, say something. It is important that all thefts are reported to police, even if there is no apparent evidence left at the scene and further investigation may not be required. Suspicious activity outside or within the building should also be reported to police.

Source: the Australian Federal Police (AFP), Australia's international law enforcement and policing representative, and the chief source of advice to the Australian Government on policing issues. More information is at **www.afp.gov.au.**

31 Sure Ways To Lower Your Operating Assets Maintenance Costs And Improve Reliability

Here is a simple checklist of 31 simple maintenance management tips that you can use to improve your operation. Use it as a guide to start you thinking which maintenance management improvement strategies to use to lower your maintenance and operational costs without spending a lot of money.

Actions for Immediately Improved Results

1. Have a lubrication regime where everything is lubricated when due and you know the right lubricant in the right condition gets all the way to where it should.

2. Have 50% of the plant or maintenance engineer's time spent out working with the plant operators and maintenance trades teaching them engineering and learning from them about the problems they have to work with.

3. Have shaft alignments done on all pumps and gearbox drives including eliminating 'soft foot'.

4. Get to know vendors and supplier's best technical people and get their advice on fixing problem plant.
5. Introduce equipment watch-keeping lists and trouble-shooting check sheets for plant operators and read them regularly to see what they notice.

6. Make plant and equipment choices and selections with a 20 to 25 year time span in mind.

7. Vibration monitor rolling bearings on critical equipment often enough to stop any failures.

8. Ask the operators and maintainers the simplest way they can think of to fix the problem.

9. Get Production and Maintenance Planners, Leading-hands and Supervisors to meet each day and prioritise the work to be done in the coming days and weeks.

Actions for Improved Results That Show Benefits for You in A Few Months' Time

1. Start measuring performance with Key Performance Indicators generated from activities and results of the business process itself. Measure both the equipment performance and the business systems' performance. Use that knowledge to continuously improve.

2. Put all Production and Maintenance Supervisors on a compulsory asset management course at diploma level.

3. Establish a basic condition-monitoring regime – process parameter tracking/ vibration/ oil condition/ thermography/ 'see-touch-hear' inspections.

4. Perform a thorough engineering review of plant changes and upgrades to make decisions based on engineering and business facts. First design and engineer, or model and simulate, or pilot- test plant changes and ideas before putting them into place permanently.
5. Go outside of the company and bring in the training and teaching that your people need to become leaders in their field.

6. Use Maintenance Planners to plan jobs in detail so you get labour efficiency and job quality.

7. Track-down all galvanic corrosion between dissimilar metals in contact and get rid of it, or monitor it closely and trend remaining life.

8. Teach operators how the equipment works and teach your maintenance trades how the production process works.

9. Provide the technical knowledge on plant and equipment your trades need, in a place they can find it fast.

10. Conduct an equipment criticality rating and match condition monitoring to the risk so you identify risk of failure in important equipment and plant.

11. Eliminate the defects - use Root Cause Analysis, 5-Whys, etc on equipment and systems failures and get the problems out forever.

12. Be proactive and imagine problems so you can solve and eliminate them before they happen.

13. Develop ownership, build skills, and build competent people at shop-floor level.

Actions for Improvements That Show You Benefits over the Coming Year or Three

1. Align the Capital Project group's output to the on-going needs of Maintenance and Operations, e.g. ensure all asset and instrument tag numbers have procurement and design information catalogued in individual files; have drawings and manuals numbered so they are easy to access for maintenance; etc.

2. Show and introduce the benefits of world class practices to managers, supervisors and leading hands. Show and introduce Corporate and Senior Managers to world class practices and methods so that can see the benefits to their 'bottom lines'

17

3. Align Operations and Maintenance efforts through a Production Plan and Schedule that covers both producing product and maintaining equipment well enough to make product.

4. Do all your statutory obligations well with full documentation and excellent procedures and practices.

5. Select the best vendors and suppliers and form a long-term partnership/alliance. This will save time, give you access to good prices, let you use their expertise to solve problems and let you focus on your business.

6. Proactively build flexibility and redundancy into the plant so you have options to address problems quickly, e.g. install tie-ins in readiness to use mobile plant if the installed item fails.

7. Apply Failure Mode and Effects Analysis and Reliability Centered Maintenance on new and old plant and equipment. On new equipment get the vendor to do the FMEA/RCM based on your industry's historical maintenance problems.

8. Select and use equipment that does not break down when it fails. Design protection into equipment that stops it breaking if it's overloaded or run wrongly. Use the grade of material that is not affected by the failure mechanism.

9. Buy equipment that can be supported and maintained locally; otherwise you will pay a lot more for parts and be waiting for service.

LRS Consultants is a network of Enterprise Asset Management, Lean Improvement, Quality Management and Maintenance Consultants for Operational Excellence, Enterprise Asset Management and World Class Reliability and Maintenance Solutions. They can be found on the web at www.lifetime-reliability.com.

8 Best Techniques For Forecasting Your Production

Manufacturers need to forecast production to estimate the future demand for their products. This list summarizes the best techniques for manufacturer's to forecast production.

1. Customer Survey Forecast - Conducting a customer survey is the most direct method of forecasting production in the short-term. Customers are surveyed on their buying intentions for products at a variety of prices. The forecast is a simple method, not based on historical records, and can produce a forecast quickly.

2. Sales Force Consensus - A manufacturer's sales team has the closest contact with customers and has a unique insight into whether customers will purchase a product. The sales force consensus is a combined forecast from the members of the sales team based on their experience and what they believe each customer will purchase over a period of time.

3. Executive Committee Consensus - The committee is comprised of a knowledgeable team of company executives that have experience in manufacturing. The group will provide their opinions on a long or medium range forecast for a single or range of products. After discussion the committee will deliver a consensus with regards a production forecast.

4. Delphi Technique - The technique involves a group of experts who will be asked their opinion on the likely forecast for an item. Generally the group will make long-range forecasts for the potential sales of a new product. A manufacturer is more likely to obtain a more accurate forecast using the Delphi Technique than from traditional unstructured forecast methods.

5. Simple Average Technique – Using the simple average technique, a production forecast is based on the average value for a given period of time. A simple average is the average of product sales for previous periods. Average calculations can be are made at different intervals to reduce any errors due to seasonal variations. So instead of using the simple average of a year of sales, quarterly averages or monthly averages are taken, which can give a more realistic forecast.

6. Trend Technique - This technique is used where a pattern or trend can be determined for the demand of a product. Manufacturers can examine past and present demand data to identify any factors that cause a trend to occur. Once these factors have been established they can be analyzed to see which factors will continue to exert an influence on the demand, so an accurate production forecast can be produced.

7. Seasonal Forecast - The demand for a manufacturer's product can be affected by a seasonal trend. Manufacturers are able to identify what the seasonal variation is for a product based on historical demand data and use that to forecast future demand. Holidays and weather changes influence products that customers require so a more accurate forecast can be created by identifying one or more seasonal trends.

8. Cyclical Forecast - By reviewing historical data manufacturers can identify if the demand for their products appears to be cyclical. This means that customers will purchase items based on economic cycles that are not fixed periods rather than defined seasonal cycles. So it is possible to forecast future production needs based if certain economic conditions are forecasted to occur.

*Martin Murray can be found at **logistics.about.com**. A writer and supply chain consultant, he is the author of many books on logistics and ERP applications.*

10 Things You Should Know About Demand Planning

While supply should be both planned and managed, demand can only be planned. Demand planning encompasses a variety of business processes depending on the exact nature of the manufacturing processes, facilities and product line. Depending on circumstances, demand forecasting, capacity management, inventory management, Sales and operations planning (S&OP), bill of material construction and maintenance, routing development and maintenance, production scheduling and material requirements planning (MRP) may all be required.

1. Understanding the Demand
A very good understanding of future demand is important to most effectively manage manufacturing operations. Demand may be independent (typically finished goods sold to customers) or dependent (typically component parts of finished goods). An individual stock-keeping unit (SKU) can have independent demand, if sold as a spare part, as well as dependent demand. Both should be identified and planned for. Independent demand is forecast and actual sales indicate whether the demand was over- or under-forecast. Dependent demand is calculated through material requirements planning processes based on the bill of materials.

2. Forecasts for Supply Chain Planning
Forecasts of independent demand should be created and used for financial planning, sales management, and especially in manufacturing supply chains for driving purchasing of raw

and packaging materials and production. Forecasts can be created at any level of the product hierarchy (e.g., family, group, category, SKU, SKU-location) and at any level of the logistics hierarchy (e.g., SKU-customer location, SKU-customer, SKU-distribution center, SKU-plant). Regardless of the level the forecast was created, it needs to be at the SKU-plant level or lower for supply chain planning.

3. Using Forecasts in Manufacturing
Definitive forecasts, as opposed to guesswork or speculation, should be used for both long-term and short-term manufacturing operations planning. In the long-term, forecasts should be utilized for planning of new or expanded facilities, new manufacturing processes, equipment acquisition, and future operating days and shifts. In the short-term, forecasts should be compared with available inventory, open purchase orders, and open work orders on a period-by-period basis for determining production needs. Forecasts should also be used to purchase finished goods, raw materials, and packaging materials.

4. Forecasting Independent Demand
Forecasts should be as accurate as possible. Over-forecasting can result in overstock inventory and the potential of sale below cost or write-off. Under-forecasting can result in out-of-stock situations, which can potentially create lost sales, gross margin, customer frustration, and excess costs to rectify the situation. Forecasting independent demand is the ultimate responsibility of sales, regardless of who has past-sales data, future promotion data, new product development plans or input through collaborative processes. The most accurate forecasts of routine (non-promotion) demand are created using naive or econometric forecasting software. Basic naive forecasting applications can be remarkably inexpensive.

5. Forecast Error
Forecast accuracy is best measured by forecast error, as forecasts can be thousands of percent in error. Forecast error

should be reduced over time and is generally measured either on a total basis or a relative basis.

Both total and relative forecast error should be measured on an absolute as opposed to a net basis. Over-forecasts of one product do not offset under-forecasts of anther product. Over-forecasts in one location do not offset under-forecasts of the same SKU in another location. Absolute error captures the true difference.

6. Calculating Dependent Demand
Dependent demand is calculated from the forecast for each SKU having independent demand in a location based on that SKU's bill of material. It is then aggregated for each dependent SKU to reflect the total dependent demand across all independent SKUs for each period. It can be completed manually for simple product lines, but it is best to calculate with Material Requirements Planning (MRP) software applications.

7. Coordinating Demand With Supply
S&OP processes should be used to bridge the gap between organizational groups to coordinate demand with supply so as to minimize overstock and out-of-stock situations. They may be supported by specialized software or most often by spreadsheet analyses. S&OP processes are conceptually very attractive and have been of major benefit to manufacturers in addressing inventory issues. They are sometimes difficult to implement due to business complexity, lack of data, or limited organizational experience in collaboration between groups. The most effective S&OP processes also incorporate major suppliers.

8. SKU Stocking Policies
The decision to manufacture or purchase a SKU is relatively simple when the network has a single or very few remote locations. In that instance, a SKU should be acquired to order only when:

- The quantity needed can be acquired in less time than has been committed to the customer
- Typical customer order quantities are less than the optimal economic quantity it would be acquired if it were to be a stocked in inventory

However, when there are multiple locations in a network, the decision to stock an SKU at a particular location is based on minimizing working capital and operating expenses subject to any requirements for maximum customer delivery time.

9. Safety Stock Inventory Management
For each SKU stocked in a location, its inventory has two parts: safety stock and cycle stock. Safety stock is not planned to be consumed and serves as a hedge against under-forecasting, longer than planned lead times, and shortages of receipts. Safety stock should be based on the desired customer service level (order fill rate) and calculated periodically based on forecast error or demand variability and lead time.

10. Cycle Stock Inventory Management
Cycle stock is intended to be consumed and "cycles" through repetitive iterations of consumption and replenishment. Cycle stock can be characterized by either order quantities or mean time between replenishment for a given volume. In most instances, order quantities should be determined by minimizing the sum of annual setup/changeover costs and inventory holding costs.

*Ralph Cox is a Senior Principal for Tompkins International (*www.tompkinsinc.com*), a leader in global supply marketing. He has extensive experience in manufacturing, warehousing, logistics, inventory management, and packaging, with particular interest in improving operating performance.*

12 Steps For Implementing A Quality Management System In Your Facility

Successful organizations have figured out that customer satisfaction has a direct impact on the bottom line. Creating an environment which supports a quality culture requires a structured, systematic process. The following are steps to implementing a quality management system that will help to bring the process full circle.

1. Clarify Vision, Mission and Values

Employees need to know how what they do is tied to organizational strategy and objectives which makes it important that all employees understand where the organization is headed (its vision), what it hopes to accomplish (mission) and the operational principles (values) that will steer its priorities and decision making. Having a process to educate employees during new employee orientation and a communication process to help ensure that the mission, vision and values is always in front of the people is a major first step.

2. Identify Critical Success Factors (CSF)

Critical success factors help an organization focus on those things that help it meet objectives and move a little closer to achieving its mission. These performance based measures provide a gauge for determining how well the organization is meeting objectives.

3. Develop Measures and Metrics to Track CSF Data

Once critical success factors are identified, there needs to be measurements put in place to monitor and track progress.

This can be done through a reporting process that is used to collect specified data and share information with senior leaders. For example, if a goal is to increase customer satisfaction survey scores, there should be a goal and a measure to demonstrate achievement of the goal.

4. Identify Key Customer Group
Every organization has customers and understanding who the key customer groups are is important so that products and services can be developed based on customer requirements. The mistake a lot of organizations make is not acknowledging employees as a key customer group.

5. Solicit Customer Feedback
The only way for an organization to know how well they are meeting customer requirements is by simply asking the question. There should be a structured process to solicit feedback from each customer group in an effort to identify what is important to them. Organizations often make the mistake of thinking they know what is important to customers and ask the wrong survey questions. This this type of feedback is obtained through customer focus groups.

6. Develop Survey Tool
Next, develop a customer satisfaction survey tool that is based on finding out what is important to customers. For example, customers might care more about quality than cost but if you are developing a product and trying to keep the cost down and skimping on the quality, you are creating a product that might not meet the needs of the customer.

7. Survey Each Customer Group
Each customer group should have a survey customized to their particular requirements and they should be surveyed to establish baseline data on the customers' perception of current practice. This provides a starting point for improvements and demonstrates progress as improvement plans are implemented.

8. Develop Improvement Plan
Once the baseline is established you should develop an improvement plan based on customer feedback from each group. Improvement plans should be written in SMART goals format with assignments to specific staff for follow through.

9. Resurvey
After a period of time (12-18 months), resurvey key customers to see if scores have improved. Customer needs and expectations change over time so being in-tune to changing needs and expectations is critical to long-term success.

10. Monitor CSF
It is important to monitor CSF monthly to ensure there is consistent progress toward goals. This also allows for course correction should priorities and objectives change during the review period.

11. Incorporate Satisfaction Data into Marketing Plans
Once you've achieved some positive results with your satisfaction data, use it as a marketing tool! A lot of successful organizations miss the boat by not letting others know what they do well. Customers want to know how an organizations internal processes work especially if those process help to deliver an outstanding product or service!

12. Technology
Make sure technology is user-friendly and supports targeted improvements. For example, a website should be easy to navigate as well as easy to find (SEO) and the content should be easy to understand.

Patricia Lotich is the founder of Thriving Small Business (thethrivingsmallbusiness.com). Patricia is a Certified Manager of Quality and Organizational Excellence through the American Society for Quality which facilitates the prestigious Malcolm Baldrige National Quality Award.

10 Performance Metrics Every Manufacturer Should Know

Every manufacturer should periodically calculate, report and review performance results that permit month-to-month and same time last year comparisons to ensure continuous improvement. When a parameter's performance reaches a structural plateau (i.e., no further improvement can be made without capital investment), a different parameter needs to replace it. If performance results are not impacted by underlying operating issues, the parameter that was measured needs to be changed to one or more underlying parameters. In no particular order, this list explores the most important performance results to manage.

1. Capacity Utilization
A clear understanding of manufacturing capacities and their utilization in various business circumstances is fundamental to best practice manufacturing management. Knowledge of capacity utilization is critical for making the best decisions about personnel, schedules, and operating shifts, as well as facilities and equipment investments.

2. Adherence to Production Schedules
The inability to adhere to production schedules is a key indicator of underlying issues that need to be understood and addressed. Being unable to follow one's own schedule can indicate a lack of understanding of manufacturing operations, the raw material supply chain or customer expectations. Understanding all three of these aspects is crucial to successful manufacturing management.

3. Labor Cost Variances

Labor cost variances are very important, but often receive the wrong attention because of absorption accounting. When manufacturing operations are under-absorbed, the action often taken is to run more of something that is not needed. Not only can this create financial issues, but the approach makes overall absorption figures look better while problematic individual products remain unchanged. This does nothing to improve manufacturing performance. When under-absorption exists, a better approach is to look at specific products where there is an opportunity to improve productivity or a need to reestablish standard cost.

4. Customer Service

Customer service can be measured in many ways, however the two most common are by order fill rates (what was shipped as a percent of what was ordered) and on-time shipment (extent to which product was shipped when the customer wanted it). Order fill rates need to be based on customer orders, not just in-stock stock keeping units (SKUs). The basis for customer shipment dates needs to be what the customer originally requested, not what was negotiated or subsequently committed.

5. Inventory Turnover (or Periods of Supply On Hand)

When inventory turnover declines or periods of supply on hand increase, several things happen. Budgeted expenses increase, profits are reduced and alternative uses for capital (which would have provided meaningful return) are eliminated. Inventory is both an asset (manufacturing lines do not have to be changed every time an order is received) and an actual or potential liability (when good product is lost, damaged, out-of-date and/or has no demand). While more simplistic than other financial performance measures such as working capital turnover or GMROI (Gross Margin Return on Inventory), it is important.

6. Employee Turnover

Low levels of employee turnover are usually circumstantial, however higher rates or increasing rates may be indicative of an employment aspect that needs to be addressed. It is always important to monitor this, even if only informally.

7. SKU Profitability

Total trailing multiple period gross margin, divided by the current number of SKUs, is an effective way to understand the financial impact of SKU proliferation. When robust processes are not in place to effectively make SKU discontinuation decisions, product lines almost always tend to drift increasingly larger, hurting profits.

8. Safety

Regardless of how they are reported, safety incident occurrence rates of all magnitudes need to be understood and addressed. The Occupational Safety and Health Administration's (OSHA) Incident Rate Calculator is a well-accepted technique. Results should be reported with enough "drill down" capability to see what is really happening—whether it be by building, line, process or shift.

9. Material Cost Variances

Material cost variances can be subtle in their ability to drain profit. Variances need to be reported at a high enough level that trends are not hidden in large amounts of detailed data. At the same time, the reporting level should not be so high that issues cannot be spotted. Achieving both simultaneously can be a challenge. Units of measure may need to be made smaller so losses are not hidden and can be more easily identified.

10. Your Biggest Issue

Whatever your biggest issue happens to be, it is important to measure, report and review results on it to continuously improve your competitiveness.

Ralph Cox *is a Senior Principal for Tompkins International (*www.tompkinsinc.com*), a leader in global supply marketing. He has extensive experience in manufacturing, warehousing, logistics, inventory management, and packaging, with particular interest in improving operating performance.*

5 Ways To Measure Your Facility's Operational Excellence

Can only the top 20% of manufacturers truly be operating at a level of operational excellence? Or, theoretically, could all operations be performed in an "excellent" manner?

One way to better address this question is to establish a set of criteria as an evaluation metric. A company's ability to score well on each attribute would suggest a high degree of operational excellence. Here are the criteria I would suggest:

1. **How collaborative is your enterprise?**
How well do you work together within departments as well as across plants? How easy is it to solicit feedback from peers in other regions, or from simply down the hall? Those organizations that have instilled a sense of 'social' in how they operate tend to deliver greater results, contributing to a higher achievement of operational excellence.

2. **What levels of process governance exist?**
This is a far-reaching topic, as it impacts not only regulatory and corporate compliance initiatives, but also to your firm's ability to effectively implement Lean manufacturing, Six Sigma and other continuous improvement programs. If processes are inconsistent and improvement can't be readily identified, improved and replicated across your organization, it will be difficult to truly achieve "excellence" status.

3. **How agile are you?**
This is another one of those terms that is often used but seldom specifically defined. I am referring to an

organization's ability to change quickly to new market opportunities, demand shifts, supply chain disruptions as well as simply the need to re-tool operations. How tough is this for you to accomplish? Does it take hours, or months? Based on what measure you use to accomplish change, you can then score yourself on how responsive your organization actually is.

4. **Do you have a culture of innovation?**
I know … another one of those vague terms. Here I am referring to not only an ability to consistently deliver new products to market that serve new needs, but also an organization's ability to think creatively to solve business issues, such as resource constraints, economic down turns or labor shortages. Those that have a good track record of innovative thoughts and processes to address these challenges score well in this criterion.

5. **How well do you operate on a global scale?**
This factor encompasses a company's ability to design, build, distribute and service anywhere. It is one thing to operate one plant and service one market. It is a completely different animal to do so effectively across locations, geographies, cultures and regulatory environments. Those organizations with a platform for manufacturing operations management that can track and trace materials, processes and resources on a global scale will be more readily capable of achieving a higher degree of operational excellence.

John Fishell manages product management, training and quality assurance teams for Apriso, a manufacturing software provider of the award-winning FlexNet software, making sure FlexNet is "ready for prime" time and includes all of the features required by Apriso's customers. Apriso's manufacturing blog can be found at www.apriso.com/blog/.

9 Ways To Reduce Your Manufacturing Overheads

The lifeblood of any business is its cash flow—that steady stream of dollars and cents that comes from sales and then flows out in the form of wages, inventory, rent, insurance and other expenses. Unfortunately, there are times when there's more "out" than "in," and only sheer perseverance keeps entrepreneurs trying to close the gap instead of closing the doors. Here's some of the more time-tested ways to keep overhead low.

1. Target overstocks.
By comparing (a) how many of each item were sold in an inventory year with (b) the item's end-of-year inventory, you can come up with what items are potentially overstocked. Next, list the overstocked items that are selling well enough to warrant holding the excess. Finally, list the overstocked items that would be worth selling at a discount to recover the cash.

2. Add up the little things.
Just in Time inventory management may be your most important way to reduce overhead, but don't ignore the smaller items that can add up to significant amounts. One approach is to list your overhead costs in descending order of expense. The result is a prioritized list of which costs to examine first to see if they can be reduced. Don't dismiss any item as "impossible to reduce" until you've scrutinized it carefully and involved your staff in looking for new options.

3. Review employee costs.
Analyze results, not efforts, to gauge which employees should stay where they are, which should be retrained, and

which should be let go. Determine your ideal number of employees by comparing your needs during your slackest times with your average days. Staff for your minimum needs as long as that level will not compromise service most of the time. It's less costly to pay overtime or bring in temporary help during peak periods than to keep unnecessary employees on the payroll.

4. Look at your facilities.
Compare your rent with what you might pay if you moved, and then ask your current landlord if your lease can be renegotiated. If you are willing to sign a longer lease, you may get a price break now or have the rent forgiven or deferred in your slowest months. Also consider shrinking the area you occupy and subleasing some of the remaining space. If you own your building, ask your banker about refinancing at a lower interest rate or over a longer term.

5. Adjust the heating and cooling of your office.
How you heat and cool your office and work space can also make a difference in your overhead costs. Questioning abnormally high bills, adding insulation, replacing old air conditioners with high-efficiency models, and wrapping hot water heaters, are steps that work for businesses as well as homes. Converting to fluorescent lighting will garner considerable savings.

6. Shop for cheaper insurance.
Rates vary widely, but so do the products and services when it comes time to make a claim. Know precisely what you are getting in a particular policy, and deal with an "A-" (or better) rated company.

7. Track responses to your advertising and promotional efforts.
To spend your advertising dollars effectively, you need to know what produces leads, and what generates profitable sales. For example, several special-category Yellow Page ads may pull better than a single large ad under your major listing.

8. Owning your phones.
Owning your phones is usually more advantageous than renting especially when you put the savings into phone services that provide more effective operation. Investigate the different services available for both local and long distance calls. Ask about volume discounts for certain time periods, to particular geographical areas, and to specific phone numbers.

9. Take a hard look at other costs.
Keep only the dues and subscriptions that serve you with valuable information or raise your profile in your industry or community. An expensive golf membership has to be evaluated in terms of whether your income would drop without it. And while you're on the golf course, ask your friends about what they're doing to reduce overhead. Networking can find you a better bookkeeper, a less expensive janitorial service or a tip for trimming your inventory still further so that your business is buoyantly afloat and doing well when the economic tide turns.

U.S. Small Business Administration (www.sba.gov)

5 Ways To Advance Lean Manufacturing With Real-time Intelligence

The necessary technology now exists, and is increasingly being used by manufacturers and their suppliers, to apply greater automation through the use of real-time information as part of a Lean manufacturing strategy. Interestingly, the full potential of the "The Toyota-Style Information System," as Taiichi Ohno envisioned it, is finally being realized today. Here are five specific ways this new-found real-time capability can be used to take Lean manufacturing to a new level:

1. **Leverage second order information** – Dynamic data, such as the up-to-the-minute or up-to-the-second standard deviation, micro-trends and variability can now be used to trigger better actions and control processes (such as dynamic buffers, dynamic Kanban flow, real-time TOC). These data can of course be used to support Six-sigma improvement efforts and reduce DMIAC cycle time for projects, as well as to improve the accuracy of master data in planning systems (standard lead time, standard cost, etc).

2. **Extend in-process visibility/intelligence for enterprise operations decision support** – This is different from typical batch-based business intelligence or after-the-fact analysis. Real-time in-process visibility enables prompt human decision-making, in effect putting executives in direct control of the manufacturing "steering wheel". While executives do not need to know all the real-time details in operation, this capability is especially important when dealing with a critical event in the

supply chain, such as during a natural disaster or an unplanned failure of a bottleneck machine.

3. **Enable pull process to supply chain partners and customers** – Synchronization of suppliers and sales is key to Lean initiatives, even when most Lean improvement efforts are focused within the four walls of a production facility. Only by coordinating in real-time with outside upstream and downstream partners can manufacturers approach the full potential of Lean practices.

4. **Sustain Kaizen** – Kaizen drives many small steps of change in the Lean journey. The effect of the small changes in shop floor layout, work sequence, equipment, methods, people and material can all now be captured and made available in real-time. This makes possible rapid measurement of Kaizen results and the benchmarking of operational KPIs across multiple facilities to reinforce common goals.

5. **Increase process and supply network flexibility** – Real-time data, if coupled with the ability to act, opens up the possibility for new levels in process and supply network flexibility. Companies now have the information they need to make decisions about ramping up suppliers, switching processes and reconfiguring supply networks to meet changing conditions.

Harnessing real-time information in these ways is not just possible, it's becoming more and more practical and cost-effective. In some industries, it's becoming a financial and competitive imperative. Today is nearly 25 years after Taiichi Ohno's seminal book, and we *finally* have the technologies to unleash the full potential of Lean methodology. This accomplishment was beyond the reach of its inventor, but it's now within ours.

James Mok *is a strategist, evangelist, consultant, project manager and implementer for Apriso. He has experience with enterprise software in manufacturing in automotive, high-tech, electronics, industrial, consumer goods and healthcare sectors. Around here we just call him "the Lean guy." Apriso's manufacturing blog can be found at http://www.apriso.com/blog/. James also has a personal blog at http://jmok007.wordpress.com.*

10 Most Important Aspects For Managing Your Plant's Manufacturing Capacity

Understanding manufacturing capacity is basic to operating expense control and is critical to customer service in times of high demand. This list summarizes the most important elements needed to define and manage manufacturing capacity.

1. Instantaneous Production Rates (and Cycle Times for Batch Operations)

Instantaneous, machine nameplate or line rates should reflect the production rate on a minute-to-minute basis, which can be achieved but typically not maintained over a shift. They should be used to determine optimum rates at which to run equipment, but generally have limited use in capacity management for planning purposes. When a line is composed of multiple functions and each with its own instantaneous rate, instantaneous rates for the complete line should be defined by the lowest of the individual function rates (whether mechanical or manual). Exceptions must be made in situations where the product can be accumulated between machines.

2. Average Production Rates (and Cycle Times for Batch Operations)

Average production rates should reflect rates that can be maintained over periods longer than a few minutes— generally over complete shifts. These should typically include start-up time, breaks, clean-up/shut-down time, short durations of equipment downtime, delays, and/or other circumstance- and personnel-driven situations. They may or may not include set-up time as noted below, and should not include significant planned or unplanned line downtime. These rates can be reliably used for planning and scheduling.

3. Setup/Changeover Time
"Setup time" is clock time for capacity management purposes as opposed to total labor time. Setup time can be handled in capacity management either explicitly or implicitly. When setup times are long or when product run lengths vary significantly, it is important to define and schedule setup time explicitly. When setup time is a small percentage of run time or when production run lengths are not significantly different, setup time can be incorporated into the average production rates successfully. It is important to ensure the fact is documented to avoid future misunderstanding.

4. Days and Operating Shifts
Capacity should be defined for a specific work plan, i.e., the number of days and shifts it is based on. The best approach is to define capacity for a single shift operation, such as five shifts per week, even when the operation normally operates two or three shifts per day, five or seven days per week. This ensures the capacity does not change even when the work plan changes. When defining capacity, it is important to document the work basis on which it is determined to avoid future misunderstandings.

5. Downtime
While short durations of unplanned downtime should normally be incorporated into average production rates (as noted above), planned downtime and longer periods of unplanned downtime should not be. Instead, planned downtime and longer periods of unplanned downtime should be taken into account to define capacity over longer periods rather than individual shifts, based on past downtime records or estimates.

6. Consumed, Committed, and Available Capacity

At any point in time, past capacity has been consumed, some future capacity has been committed, and some future capacity is available. Past capacity that has been consumed should be evaluated in terms of actual production as a percent of capacity resulting in utilization. It is important to understand utilization—by plant, by line, by shift—for future planning and production scheduling. Determining how to commit future capacity in the best way is an important order management issue.

7. Fixed and Flexible Capacity

In many operations, some capacities are essentially fixed and some may be flexible, generally by adding temporary personnel or overtime. When defining capacity, it is important to document the fixed/flexible basis on which it is determined to avoid future misunderstandings.

8. Short-term Future Demand

Excess short-term demand is demand that is forecast to occur a few weeks or months ahead for which capacity is not available. When capacity is fixed, or when the demand cannot be shifted to another operation, the issue should be addressed by manufacturing in excess of current requirements for a period of time and pre-building inventory for the subsequent demand. The amount of inventory needed to cover the over-capacity period can be determined by completing a period-by-period plan of inventory, production, and shipments, cascading the manufacturing for future demand back in time until capacity permits its manufacture.

9. Long-term Future Demand: Equipment vs. Operating Days and Shifts

While excess short-term demand must be accommodated, excess long-term demand should be planned for. It is generally planned for by adding production capacity/shift or by adding operating shifts. At the most simple level, the solution lies in the economics of the options. However, a more comprehensive approach should take into account labor availability, space availability, capital funds availability, nighttime noise when neighborhoods are nearby and other factors.

10. Production Scheduling

Capacity is used to develop plans for production of specific work orders for specific quantities of specific products during specific future periods. Schedules should be rigid enough to satisfy customers, but also flexible enough to allow costs to be minimized. For production scheduling purposes, capacity can unfortunately be overstated (vs. the truth), which creates waiting time and associated cost issues. In addition, capacity can also unfortunately be understated (also vs. the truth), which creates customer service or overtime issues. Understanding actual capacity and what drives under- or over-utilization is an important function of manufacturing management.

*Ralph Cox is a Senior Principal for Tompkins International (*www.tompkinsinc.com*), a leader in supply chain consulting and integration. He has extensive experience in manufacturing, warehousing, logistics, inventory management, and packaging, with particular interest in improving operating performance.*

5 Ways A Manufacturer Can Cut Energy Use

Manufacturers can target five areas that could have the greatest overall effect on their facilities' energy efficiency.

1) Use free cooling: In the winter, companies can use a heat exchanger to take advantage of cool outside temperatures, to chill water, valves and control modifications.

2) Waste heat recovery: Excess heat from cooling towers, exhaust and boiler flue gas can be used for space or process heat. Such heat can often be recovered using a simple air duct and summer/winter damper. Heat recovery provides an enticing opportunity for industries using gas compression processes, according to a recent story in Sustainable Plant. About 50,000 Btu/hr of thermal energy is available to be recovered for every 100 cfm of air provided during compression.

3) Reduce peak energy use: Companies should record their electric loads and average the power use to determine peak loads and re-time operations accordingly.

4) Optimize air compressors' efficiency by base-loading all but one compressor. This "swing machine" maintains system pressure.

5) Turn off equipment when not in use: Monitor equipment for a week to see when it's not being used. Also, consider electrical system modeling.

*InBalance LLC (*inbalancebuildings.com*) is an engineered energy efficiency solutions firm specializing in industrial and large commercial facilities.*

7 Important Zoning Law Considerations Every Manufacturer Should Know

Your business may not be as free to do everything that you think. You'll need to be careful that your activities don't violate your local government's zoning regulations. You'll also need to keep this in mind when purchasing property too. What are some important zoning law considerations? Here are a few.

1. Know the definition of zoning - Zoning ordinances regulate, by districts, the uses of land and buildings for trade, industry, residence, and other purposes. the purpose of zoning is to protect the public's health, safety, morals, and general welfare. by enacting zoning ordinances, state and local governments limit the size, height, density, and types of buildings to be erected; regulate areas of open spaces, yards, and courts; and regulate and restrict the location of trades, industries, and buildings.

2. Find out about your zoning district - Boundaries are established for each zoning district. a municipality is divided into various types of districts that permit agricultural use, one-family residential use, two-family residential use, industrial use, business use, trailer camp and park use, or open-space use. Each municipality has its own system of classifying zoning districts. a residential use, for example, in one municipality may permit professionals or certain business offices to operate out of a home.

3. Know about retroactivity - Zoning laws are not retroactive. a building in existence at the time a zoning law is adopted cannot be declared illegal. But if the illegal structure is destroyed, the owner may rebuild only in accordance with present zoning laws without substantially enlarging the building.

4. Determine if there is a variance on your property - A variance authorizes a landowner to use property in a manner forbidden by the zoning ordinance if the zoning creates particular difficulties or unnecessary hardships. the two categories are area variances and use variances. an area variance affects the size of the property, such as a one-acre variance sought by a landowner who owns 1.9 acres and sells one lot, leaving him with 0.9 of an acre. a use variance affects how land can be used in a particular neighborhood, such as the use of property for a gasoline station in a residential neighborhood. an application for a use variance must show that the zoning law imposes an undue hardship.

5. Know what's involved for a change in use - For a change of use, the owner may be required to show a special hardship that is, proof in the form of dollars and cents that the property does not yield a reasonable return. the owner-applicant is required to show that the land cannot yield a reasonable return if used only for the purpose allowed in that zone, the owner's plight is due to unique circumstances and not to the general conditions in the neighborhood, and the use to be authorized by the variance will not alter the locality's essential character. If your application for a variance is rejected, you may appeal to the courts.

6. Make sure you're not subject to unconstitutional zoning - Zoning regulations must be reasonable, uniform, and not unduly oppressive to landowners. If a zoning ordinance unreasonably restricts the uses of a district, it can be attacked as being unconstitutional. There must be specific damage, however, to bring such a lawsuit. Although a landowner does not have to own property actually situated within the zoned area, the land must be adversely affected by the zoning law.

Zoning is constitutional if reasonable consideration has been given to the character of the district, its suitability for a particular use, the conservation of property values, and well-planned building development.

7. **Always check with an attorney** - If you plan to alter property you are buying or use it for a business, check with an attorney before signing the purchase contract to determine whether you will be walking into a zoning law problem.

Robert Friedman, attorney and author of various legal guides. the Upstart Small Business Legal Guide has been published on the websites of USA Today, BusinessWeek, FindLaw, CBS-TV, Fox-TV and the LA Daily News. How to Survive Legally as a Landlord and Injury Victim's Legal Survival Guide have been published in Thomson-West's Am Jur Trials. Contact him at Robert Friedman at (800) 729-4571 or e-mail him at rfriedman@legalsurvival.com.

Chapter 2: Your Inventory

10 Steps For Implementing A Material Handling System

The distribution center (DC) is a key asset to a company's overall logistics strategy. The design of material handling systems within the DC (e.g., conveyors, sorters, storage/retrieval systems) and the way those components are integrated into a company's IT system can have a major impact on customer service, customer satisfaction and overall profitability. This list illustrates important topics to consider when planning a new material handling system for a business.

1. Partner with an integration professional.
Equipment manufacturers represent themselves as one stop design and integration resources. Although well-intentioned, they may not necessarily be trained to evaluate a business's logistics needs served by the DC, collect and analyze operational data, and to look for the optimal solution using best of breed products for a company's needs. Partnering with a materials handling systems integrator offers the benefit of an objective solution (regardless of manufacturer) that is designed with the sole objective to serve the company's needs.

2. Gather current and historical data for DC design.
DC material handling design begins with current operational data. It is extremely important to understand the product mix, staging, reserve storage, inbound receiving, picking, conveyability, cartonization, consolidation, palletizing and shipping strategies that need to be serviced by the material

handling system. As in all business solutions, if someone begins with the wrong data, they cannot have correct results.

3. Apply predictive modeling and scenario thinking to refine the design.

In the past, it was sufficient to take an existing business model and apply a five year growth projection. This resulted in a satisfactory requirement for the distribution strategy and choice of material handling capability (e.g., architecture, throughput, system layout). However, the current reality is that businesses are increasingly faced with disruptive innovation. Companies need to run modeling projections on different business scenarios to adequately prepare for the future. For example, current data and a business model may result in a DC design that is optimized for pallet shipments to retailers. What would happen if customers implemented a more frequent restocking model? What would happen if single carton shipping requirements increased dramatically due to e-commerce initiatives? These scenarios will have a dramatic effect on material handling choices within the DC.

4. Fix inefficient processes.

A data analysis and predictive modeling/scenario thinking exercise will most likely lead to a fresh perspective on how things are (and have always been) conducted. Resist temptation to simply automate an outdated and inefficient process. Exception processing in particular can drive high equipment expense. Take the opportunity to streamline processes and achieve efficiency wherever possible. This approach is often called, "More thought, less iron" because of its potential to reduce overall capital investment in material handling equipment (MHE).

5. Build preplanned expansion points into the design.

MHE design can be "future proofed" by building in a preplanned expansion capability to address possible future scenarios. This means choosing equipment layouts that preplan for expansion needs. For example: Identifying where a second pick module may be needed and ensuring the packing sorter is not in that location. Instead, use the area for easily moved operations. It may mean a modest investment in discrete components now (such as additional merge and divert conveyor modules) that will eliminate the need for system cut-ins and work stoppages during a future expansion project.

6. Design for IT connectivity.
Modern material handling controls are information-rich sources of actionable data. The MHE system is no longer just a way to move boxes around a DC. It is now the source of valuable supply chain data for the company and its customers. Recognize that mobile connectivity and real-time status updates are increasingly expected by internal decision makers as well as customers. Add flexibility to MHE IT architecture by choosing a warehouse control system to address the gaps in the warehouse management system and enterprise resource planning. A warehouse control system is the software layer that connects MHE equipment to the company's overall IT strategy.

7. Develop a structured test plan.
Successful material handling system integration requires an ability to anticipate and manage the challenges of physical, electrical and information system installation and testing. Use the design phase of the project to develop a test plan that addresses all key schedule milestones and critical business assumptions. One area of particular concern is the integration of IT systems to the MHE equipment. Test IT messaging and data flow as early in the process as possible. Insist on a simple proof of concept messaging test during the software build process (even as the physical conveyor is just beginning to roll off the manufacturer's assembly line) to ensure all parties are working to the same IT specifications and requirements.

8. Allow time for the "ramp up" and "go live" phases of the project.
Bringing a new material handling system online is typically a major change to a company's customary operation. Allow time in the project schedule to ramp up the shipping volume and work out any of the initial problems with processes and equipment.

9. Build in time for adequate training of the DC workforce.
A modern material handling system will often place increased demands on the workforce to interact with information systems. For example, associates may need to respond to voice-directed picking, and supervisors may need to use new reporting systems to manage and optimize the workload. Build in time and resources for adequate training of the DC workforce prior to "go live." Continue this training support during the critical first weeks of go live to reinforce the correct processes within the DC.

10. Use the new capabilities to optimize business effectiveness.
The intelligence of modern MHE systems allows users to collect data, analyze DC key process indicators against business assumptions, and make adjustments to staffing, hours and work practices as needed to achieve desired results. Do not lose sight of these advantages in the daily rush to get product shipped out the door. Establish regular reviews of the data (daily, weekly, and quarterly reviews) to ensure the investment in material handling systems yields the desired productivity returns.

*Kelly Reed is a Partner for Tompkins International (*tompkinsinc.com*). Kelly has over 30 years' experience in logistics, warehousing, warehouse management systems, material handling systems, inventory management, and inventory deployment.*

10 Ways Managing Your Inventory Will Improve Your Customer Service

Focusing on the right things in inventory management to improve customer service can be a challenging and daunting task. However, there are basic strategies every company can employ to ensure your inventory is customer-centric. By doing so, this important asset can be leveraged to your business' advantage. Here are ten tips to help you begin in the right direction.

1. Keep inventory records accurate.
Inventory records need to be current and up to date. Inaccurate record keeping can cause embarrassing customer service issues. Not only can you lose the sale, but you also lose credibility. Buying more inventory of items that are already in excess supply does nothing for service, while on the contrary, needed items that are missing causes production delays or excessive and costly expediting. Consider instituting a cycle count program for keeping records current and driving out process errors that cause inventory inaccuracy.

2. Keep supplier lead times current and up to date.
Excessive stock outs can be caused by something as simple as not ordering at the right time. By making sure lead times are correct, you will reduce your chances of a stock out and improve customer service.

3. Know your incremental inventory carrying costs.
Carrying costs are one of the main components affecting the cost to serve. Variable costs (e.g., opportunity cost or

outright cost of capital, taxes and insurance, handling costs) are important to everyday purchase decisions. Buyers need to use incremental carrying costs to determine whether or not a given volume discount will make good financial sense and can be passed on to customers.

4. Know your incremental inventory transaction costs.
Like incremental carrying costs, inventory transaction costs have a strong effect on the cost to serve. Incremental transaction costs, such as variable labor for additional purchase order creation, confirmation and expediting, receipt and invoice payment, and freight costs are important to creating inventory policies that make good financial sense. Incremental transaction costs guide the decision on how often to buy and how much to buy.

5. Base cycle stock levels on economics.
Buying too much will increase carrying costs, while buying too frequently will increase transaction costs. The right approach is to find the optimal amount to order by balancing carrying and transaction costs to find the lowest total cost of the two combined. Lowering your total cost to serve will provide savings that can be passed on to customers.

6. Calculate safety stocks according to desired customer service levels.
Use a statistic-based approach to determine the right level of safety stock for your target customer service levels. Determining the right level to achieve your goals will reduce stockouts, eliminate excess inventory, and drive revenues through improved fill rates.

7. Stratify your inventory.
One size does not fit all when it comes to the way you handle stocking policies. The best way to stratify for customer service is by hits or how frequently customers buy an item. Segregate items using an ABC analysis and set safety stock policies appropriate to each class to optimize overall fill rate performance.

8. Manage your excess and obsolete inventory.
Having space and capital tied up in excess or obsolete inventory will lessen your ability to have those resources dedicated to the items your customers need. Create an appropriate excess and obsolete reserve and take action on a regular basis to use it.

9. Track lost sales.
Be sure your fill rate data includes opportunities missed. Customer service will improve if you keep an accurate accounting of the items you were not available to sell and the reasons why. Acting on these discoveries can help you get the sale next time.

10. Improve forecast accuracy by editing out and adding back in.
One-time events, such as promotions and spikes in demand, need to be edited out of history to produce reliable results. Once a base forecast has been established, add back future promotions or sales lifts and demand for any lost sales. Anticipating and planning for the future will improve your customer service going forward.

Vince Esposito is a Principal in Global Supply Chain Services for Tompkins International (tompkinsinc.com). With over 30 years of supply chain management experience in distribution and manufacturing, Vince is an expert in Supply Chain Network Design, Transportation Management, Distribution/ Fulfillment Center Design and Implementation, Forecasting and Inventory Management, Procurement, and Supply Chain Due Diligence.

20 Methods For Reducing Your Overstocked Inventory

Overstocked inventory happens for a number of reasons. Here are fun ways to reduce these levels:

1. Return for credit.

2. Allocate to a new, more in demand product.

3. Sell at a discount to another company that uses the same material.

4. Look at the finished products list for ideas that are appropriate to the raw materials you have an excess of.

5. Contact customers who have ordered this product in the past and offer them a bulk discount.

6. Discount steeply while product still has demand.

7. Barter: barter directly with customers for products or services you want from them, or find a barter company on the Internet.

8. Hold a 2-for-1 sale.

9. Write off on your taxes as a loss.

10. Donate to a charity to take tax write off – see accountant for the tax rules; this might be better than an extreme discount.

11. Give to your best customers to use for giveaways to bring in retail customers.

12. Contact manufacturers reps to offer exceptional pricing.

13. Bundle with something else to create a package that is still valuable.

14. Find a new market.

15. Run an ad in commercial directories – free or paid.

16. Sell to closeout retail chains.

17. Sell to online discount retailers.

18. Sell at a flea market, especially if your overstock inventory is relatively small.

19. Advertise on online auctions sites and online classified advertising sites.

20. Set up an account on Amazon, provided the product still has retail value.

John R. Aberle worked and consults with and for businesses from Fortune 100 companies down to a small computer dealership. For more information go to AberleEnterprises.com.

8 Best Ways To Reduce Your Overall Inventories

Excess inventory hurts the company in several ways. It ties up cash, which could be used more productively in paying down debt or pursuing alternative opportunities. It takes up space, forcing you to add onto your facility, and uses unnecessary leased space. Excess inventory can increase your insurance and taxes. It exposes you to risks associated with shrinkage, obsolescence, and damage related to excess handling. Here are some of the steps you can take to get your inventory under control:

1. Evaluate your inventory control "infrastructure." - If you haven't already, is it time to automate inventory control? If you are using a management software package, is the inventory control module adequate for your needs? Do your processes support the keeping of inventory counts that are accurate and timely? Is your inventory layout conducive to administering "real-time" inventory control?

2. Perform a cost-benefits analysis on an increased commitment to inventory control. - Can your staff take on the extra duties involved? While getting such a system going can require a lot of initial attention, inventory control systems save time in the longer run, by allowing you to know what's in stock without having to go to the warehouse, by quickly detecting any possible theft, and by lowering rates of stock-out (lost sales) and overstock.

3. Set a target for customer service level - Measures can include percent of orders filled completely, or items delivered as a percent of items ordered. The primary constraint on reducing inventory is, of course, customer service level. What's an acceptable service level for you? 95%? 99.5%? Inventory control software generally uses such a figure to determine how much "safety stock" you need to meet this objective.

4. Implement cycle counting - To make a system work well you have to be committed to keeping accurate inventory on a real-time basis, which necessitates "cycle counting." Cycle counting is an inventory management procedure where a small subset of inventory is counted on any given day. Instead of taking a physical inventory once a year, for example, you can say count 2% (one-fiftieth) of your inventory each week up to the fiftieth week of the year. Using this method errors are caught more quickly, and extra counts can be performed on error-prone items.

5. Implement Just-in-Time - JIT includes a set of actions that work together to squeeze slack out of your processes. Do you enter received material as soon as it arrives? Can your key suppliers commit to shorter lead times?

6. Identify overstock items - Identify overstock items in your Inventory control system. Sometime the inventory may go straight to the trash heap, but some may be sent back to the manufacturer. You may want to think about having a garage sale and selling or donating the rest to a local housing agency.

7. Analyze contribution of each item in inventory - Take a hard look at the realistic contribution of every item in inventory. You may need to keep some losers as "service items," but you will be amazed at how many of your items are break-even or worse.

8. Partner strategically - Can you narrow your number of suppliers by getting more items from the "majors?" You may currently split up orders to save a penny here and there, but the vendor left standing would probably meet or beat the other's prices for a greater share of your business. More from each vendor means more frequent replenishment, and more opportunities for Just-in-Time.

Dr. John B. Vinturella, *Vinturella and Associates, (www.jbv.com). Dr. Vinturella has almost 40 years' experience as a management and strategic consultant and entrepreneur, and 15 of those years as an academic Entrepreneur-in-Residence and Adjunct Professor. Dr. Vinturella is co-author of "Raising Entrepreneurial Capital"* (Elsevier, 2004), *and author of "The Entrepreneur's Fieldbook"* (Prentice Hall, 1999).

6 Great Ways To Better Store Your Inventory

Storing inventory is more than just putting things in a warehouse; it's about finding the right place for everything and making the best use of your storage space. To get the most out of your inventory, you should use an inventory storage method that fits well with the types of products you sell. You can even combine some of these methods, depending on your needs.

1. By popularity

Rank all of your products by how many you sell over a certain period of time. Then put your top-selling products closest to the receiving door of your warehouse and work your way down the list to store the rest farther away. This is a simple yet effective way to organize your inventory and reduce the amount of time it takes to fill orders and receive items.

2. By group

If you sell a number of products that fall into the same category, group them all together in the same area. This makes it easier to find cleaning agents, electronics, and virtually anything else based on what they are.

3. By combination

There are many products that complement other products, making them popular to buy in conjunction (e.g., potato chips and soft drinks, sunglasses and suntan lotion, cookies and milk). By storing these products next to each other, even if they are in completely different categories, you can save time and be more efficient in your picking process.

4. By size

Large items are often more expensive and more difficult to move than smaller items. Thus, it can be practical to keep bigger products closer to the receiving door in order to minimize transportation risks within the warehouse. Grouping items by size can also make the task of finding items in the warehouse more intuitive.

5. By cost

Generally, more expensive items will be sold less frequently than cheaper items, so it may be a good idea to organize your inventory by price range and store cheaper products in easy-to-access locations.

6. By expiration date

Food manufacturers, restaurants, grocery stores, and other businesses that go through a lot of perishable products each day should take their expirations dates into account when storing them. For example, dairy items, breads, fruits, vegetables, and other products with short freshness periods should be stored in a way that makes them easy to restock on a regular basis. This helps prevent spoilage and other waste.

Robert Lockard, *(*fishbowlinventory.com*). A prolific writer, he is the author of hundreds of articles and blog posts on inventory management and other business topics. Fishbowl Inventory is the No. 1 inventory management software for small and midsize businesses using QuickBooks.*

4 Ways To Keep Your Inventory Lean

It's important to note that keeping inventory low isn't necessarily the best strategy for every business. The amount of inventory a business should have on hand should be based on a variety of factors. In a perfect world businesses would always have exactly enough inventory to meet demand. Keeping inventory too low could lead to a loss in sales because of shortages. On the other hand, having too much inventory could result in wasted money due to tied-up cash, decreased margins, and high carrying costs.

1. Categorize inventory using ABC codes - The ABC code process would essentially allow you to organize parts based on their importance.

A Part would be the most important to keep track of and would have more frequent purchasing intervals. Example: 1-week supply, purchased weekly. B Parts would be less important and would have slightly longer purchasing intervals. Example: 2-week supply, purchased bi-weekly. C Parts are the least important and would have the longest purchasing intervals or they would be only purchased as needed for open orders. Example: 4-week supply, purchased every 4 weeks.

2. Use just in time purchasing - During different processes there would be a notification on when to order an item. An example of just in time purchasing process would be a business that has production that is scheduled a month in advance and a purchase order would done to buy everything that is needed for the next two weeks. This reduces the carrying costs of inventory because it only sits in stock for a small amount of time.

3. Set reorder points and recalculate them often - Reorder points can be created to allow products to be flagged and reordered once they get below a specific amount in stock. Normally this is calculated as a min and a max, so they won't go above or below certain levels. The calculations for reorder points can be done based on historical data in looking at how much inventory was needed over a period of time, the number of days between purchasing, how much lead time there is from a vendor, and how much safety stock should be held.

MIN Inventory Level = (Lead Time + Safety Stock) * Unit Sales Per Day
MAX Inventory Level = Reorder Point + (Order Interval * Unit Sales Per Day)

4. Keep accurate counts and set tight control processes - Keeping accurate inventory counts when it comes to maintaining healthy inventory levels. It also helps employees and departments have more trust in the data that is in the system. If they trust that everything is accurate, then they are more likely to order exactly what they need without any excess. The data that comes out of an inventory database is only as good as the data that goes in and the processes used to keep track of the inventory. When these are properly in place, then this level of confidence can be achieved.

Malcolm Felt, *inventory solutions specialist with Fishbowl* (fishbowlinventory.com*), is a serial entrepreneur who has implemented inventory management processes for small and mid-sized businesses to divisions of publicly traded companies.*

7 Ideas For Turning Your Inventory Into Cash

With less inventory, there are lower costs of holding inventory. Here are some methods to reduce inventory and increase cash.

1. Increase demand forecasting accuracy - We only need enough inventory to satisfy demand, and that is where part of the problem exists. If demand cannot be accurately forecasted, then we end up compensating for this unknown with inventory.

2. Increase manufacturing cycle efficiency - How well manufacturing resources are used to produce a product determines the cycle efficiency. Defective product, product rework, and long lags between manufacturing cells cause inefficiency, which can be easily calculated. Raw materials should be converted into finished goods as quickly as possible. The speed at which this occurs defines your manufacturing cycle efficiency.

3. Increase supply chain turns - Increasing the number of times purchases are made may increase acquisition costs and unit costs because of smaller order quantities. But you will benefit by increasing your cash flow and eliminating the carrying cost of the inventory (warehousing, material handling, taxes, insurance, depreciation, interest and obsolescence totaling 25% to 35%).

4. Eliminate safety stock - Safety stock is really just a buffer for forecasting variance and supplier delivery time. While many levels are set arbitrarily in automated MRP systems, your safety stock levels will need to be reduced due to improvements in demand forecasting accuracy, manufacturing cycle efficiency and supply chain turns.

5. Reduce purchasing errors - This can reduce overstocking and, more importantly, minimize stock outs that result in expensive expedited purchases. Sell excess and obsolete inventory or return it to your vendor.

6. Eliminate delivery variance - Do not allow vendors to deliver early or late and make sure the delivered quantity does not vary from the order quantity. After all, delivery errors cause the need to carry more inventory. Instead, provide suppliers with forecasts of future needs.

7. Train purchasing personnel - Provide your purchasing and material management personnel with formal training. This will arm them with better negotiating skills that will result in better prices and terms.

Chris Anderson, managing director of Bizmanualz, Inc. (www.bizmanuals.com) and co-author of policies and procedures manuals, producing the layout, process design and implementation to increase performance. Anderson has over 20 years of sales, marketing and business management experience working with small to large corporations and has worked with business process design, software and systems engineering consulting with companies large and small. Contact them at Bizmanualz, Inc., 7777 Bonhomme Avenue, Suite 2222 Clayton, Missouri 63105, U.S. Toll-Free: 1-(800)-466-9953

8 Tips To Increase Your Inventory Turnover

Are you looking for ways to increase your inventory turnover? The following are some ways to increase your inventory turnover from our expert...The Ambassador Of Selling.

1. Dating from vendors - "Vendor dating" means that the vendor will hold off billing for the goods delivered for, say 60 or 90 days or they will make the invoice payable, with anticipation discount (i.e. 3% EOM) with a 60 or 90 day due date from date of delivery. One might say the goods are on consignment for that amount of time. However, the difference between vendor dating and consignment is that with the former, the bill has to be paid eventually. How does vendor dating increase turnover? Well, if the goods are ones that have been selling previously, most likely some or all of the goods will be sold before the bill has to be paid.

2. 80/20 rule - A method of a "horizontal" look at what and how much is selling when. Not only is business cyclical, but each product/service within a business is cyclical. Not everything sells well all the time and some products/services sell less often or rarely. Possibly, however, these last two categories cannot be eliminated due to the 80/20 Rule – 80% of the products/services sold are done with 20% of the selection of products/services available. A "horizontal look" at inventory usage: most inventory systems show total on-hand and sales for the previous month and to-date sales. Bit, in order to get a "horizontal picture" one would have to overlay each page of like items so it shows the relative changes month by month (or week-by-week if necessary) vs. one month at a time.) Since the 80/20 rule prevails with inventory, working on increasing the sales and rate of sale of slower selling items will help increase sale of the better selling ones. It is also a better use of one's inventory. Since the 80/20 rule prevails with inventory, working on increasing the sales and rate of sale of slower selling items will help increase sales of the better selling ones. It is also a better use of one's inventory.

3. Buy less more often - Try to buy less but more often even though buying more at one time may be less costly.

4. Consignment goods - Obtain consignment goods to back up current inventory or in addition to current inventory. The difference between vendor dating and consignment is that with the vendor dating, the bill has to be paid eventually. With consignment goods, only those goods sold have to be paid for. In addition, usually a consignment agreement says that unsold items may be returned as long as the goods and their packaging are still in saleable condition.

5. Implement "Locker Stock" program - Another way to increase inventory turnover that some vendors offer, is called a "locker stock" program. In this situation, the vendor puts goods in a store on consignment. However, the agreement says that the store and the vendor have to agree on what goods are on the display. Then, any goods sold will be replaced and the store pays for the replacement. The "catch 22" of vendor dating, locker stock or consignment is that often these goods are sold in lieu of selling goods the store already owns hence, inventory turnover is not increased. Not only that, if sales of these special programs increase and sales of owned goods stay the same or decrease, inventory turn decreases. This is the merchandise version of Newton's Law that for every force there is an equal opposite force.

6. Box-lotting - "Box-lotting" refers to taking slow(er) selling items/services with better selling ones at a combined special price.

7. Display changes – Change the display or manner of presentation or products/services so that the slower-selling ones are more prominent.

8. Closeout sales - Have closeout sales to free money for better selling items.

Alan J. Zell, the Ambassador Of Selling, has become nationally recognized for his expertise in advising businesses, services, educational, governmental, and organizational entities. Clients seeking his services represent a wide spectrum including accountants, investors, educators, chambers of commerce, retailers, wholesalers, manufacturers, associations, and non-profit organizations. Contact him at P.O. Box 69, Portland, Oregon, USA 97207-0069, 503-241-1988 or via his website at www.sellingselling.com

5 Ways To Best Leverage Your "Internet of Assets"

Plant-floor equipment must share operational status with other equipment, which might now be located in other factories at various locations. Data and intelligence requirements will only escalate, creating huge pressure to more efficiently access and understand big data now being generated by each of these plants. Obviously, this requirement might be seriously at risk if your equipment is not capable of remote management, monitoring and sharing of operational performance. Collecting and processing all this information will be essential to coordinate the global plant floor. Your operations network will become more agile and dynamic. And, it will support rapid reconfigurations of production operations, and will be able to flexibly respond faster to ever changing customer fulfillment requirements.

It is for this purpose that the "Internet of Assets" can become a real value-add.

The following technology enablers will put you on the fast track to achieving your own global plant floor, letting you best leverage your "Internet of Assets":

1. A network of intelligent sensors, devices and equipment that can share plant-specific information on a wireless network, in real time.

2. A cloud-based platform that enables those intelligent devices to interact and cooperate with people and IT applications.

3. A decision support system based on Big Data analytics that finds patterns in huge amounts of information and helps manufacturers spot trends and track issues back to their root causes.

4. Social business tools that act as a collaborative hub to enable the rapid diffusion of information, for example machines that can tweet their status.

5. Mobile applications that enable knowledge workers on the plant floor to access intelligent information in real time.

Gordon Benzie is Apriso's resident blog-master, responsible for keeping the Manufacturing Transformation blog content fresh and interesting. Apriso's manufacturing blog can be found at www.apriso.com/blog.

Chapter 3: Your People

20 Ways That The IRS Distinguishes an Employee From A Sub Contractor

Independent contractors are individuals who are in business for themselves and hire out their labor to clients. Employers are cautioned to be extremely careful not to misclassify a worker as an independent contractor as the tax consequences could be significant. When evaluating subcontractor/ employee relationships, these are the typical factors that the IRS will look at.

1. Instructions - The IRS considers a person to be an employee when they are required to comply with an employer's instructions as to how to do the job. They are considered an independent contractor when they follow their own instructions.

2. Training - The IRS considers someone to be an employee when they are required to be trained by the employer on how to do the job. They are considered an independent contractor when they do not require training from the employer.

3. Integration - The IRS considers someone to be an employee when services are fully integrated into the employer's business, which is significantly dependent upon them. They are considered an independent contractor when services are not integrated into the employer's business.

4. Personal - The IRS considers someone to be an employee when they are required to perform services personally.

5. Assistants - The IRS considers someone to be an employee when assistants are hired, supervised and paid by the employer. The IRS considers them independent when they generally hire their own assistants, required only to attain a particular result.

6. Continuity - The IRS considers someone to be an employee when there is a continuing economic relationship which may include work at recurring but irregular intervals. An independent contactor has no assumption of continuing relationship.

7. Hours of work - The IRS considers someone to be an employee when they are required to perform work within set hours of work specified by the employer. The IRS considers them an independent contractor when they are free to establish own hours of work.

8. Time required - The IRS considers someone to be an employee when they usually devote full-time to the employer's business and may be restricted from performing work for others. They are considered an independent contractor when they may work at any time and for whomever.

9. Work location - The IRS considers someone to be an employee when they perform work on the employer's premises. The IRS considers them an independent contractor when their work may be performed anywhere, often at worker's office or location.

10. Sequence of work - The IRS considers someone to be an employee when they follow orders or a sequence of work set by employer. The IRS considers them an independent contractor then are free to accomplish work in any sequence.

11. Reports - The IRS considers someone to be an employee when they generally makes regular or periodic, either oral or written, to the employer. The IRS considers them an independent contractor when they are not necessarily required to submit regular reports.

12. Payment - The IRS will consider someone to be an employee when they are generally paid by time, i.e., hour, week or month. The IRS considers someone to be an independent contractor when they are generally paid by result, i.e., completion of project or straight commission.

13. Expenses - The IRS considers someone to be an employee when they are generally reimbursed for business related expenses, implying right of regulation and direction by the employer. The IRS will consider them an independent contractor when they generally cover their own expenses and expenses may be included in total payment.

14. Tools and Materials - The IRS considers someone to be an employee when the tools and materials needed for job are provided by the employer. The IRS considers them an independent contractor when they use their own tools and materials to accomplish work.

15. Facility Investment - The IRS will consider someone to be an employee when they generally have no investment in facilities required to accomplish work, indicating dependence on the employer's facilities. The IRS will consider them an independent contractor when they have an investment in facilities, such as an office rented from third party.

16. Profit or loss - The IRS will consider someone to be an employee when they cannot realize a profit or loss on his services. The IRS will consider them an employee when they have an exposure to economic gain or loss on accomplishment of work.

17. Simultaneous work - The IRS will consider someone to be an employee when they perform work under a single financial arrangement. The IRS will consider them an independent contractor when they perform work simultaneously for multiple, unrelated persons or entities.

18. General public - The IRS will consider someone to be an employee when they do not make services available to general public. The IRS will consider them an independent contractor when they make services available to the general public on regular basis.

19. Discharge - The IRS will consider someone to be an employee when the employer can fire and thereby control nature and pace of work through threat of firing. The IRS will consider them an independent contractor when they cannot be discharged so long as result is satisfactory.

20. Termination - The IRS will consider someone to be an employee when they can quit at any time without liability. The IRS will consider them an independent contractor when they can terminate only with risk of breach of contract liability.

United States Small Business Administration (www.sba.gov)

6 Tactics For Avoiding Immigration Problems

U.S. employers must be very careful when they hire immigrants to work in the U.S. On one hand, substantial penalties can be imposed against both companies and individuals who hire people not authorized to work in this country. On the other hand, it is illegal to discriminate against immigrants who are authorized to work. Thus, employing some foreigners would violate the law, while refusing to employ others would violate the law. Our expert, an immigration law specialist, offers these tips to avoid problems.

1. Complete an I-9 form - Follow strictly the I-9 form that must be completed for each new hire. That form lists the documents that will establish an individual's authorization to work in the U.S.

2. Audit supervisors' behaviors - Audit supervisors' behaviors to ensure that they are not treating some ethnic groups differently than others.

3. Tolerate accents - Tolerate accents unless they interfere with job performance. Further, impose "English only" rules only when absolutely necessary to the job.

4. Know job requirements - Be sure height and weight requirements are necessary for the job, since foreigners may have difficulty meeting those requirements.

5. During interview, ask if he/she is authorized to work in U.S. - During job interviews, ask whether an individual is authorized to work in the United States, not whether (s)he is a U.S. citizen.

6. Obtain a copy of INS regulations - Finally, the Immigration and Nationalization Service (INS), the agency responsible for enforcement of the IRCA, has issued an extensive set of regulations implementing the Act. Employers should obtain a copy of the INS regulations because they are an excellent guideline for complying with the IRCA.

Dr. Steven E. Abraham is currently a professor in the Department of Management and Marketing, State University of New York at Oswego, where he teaches Employment Law, Labor Law, Legal & Social Environment of Business, Labor Relations and Human Resource Management. Dr. Abraham's primary research interest is the interrelationship between law and employment and he has investigated this relationship both empirically and conceptually. Contact him at the Department of Management, State University of New York at Oswego (www.oswego.edu/~abraham), 316 Rich Hall, Oswego, New York 13126, (315) 312-3307, email: abraham@Oswego.edu

6 Ways To Maximize Your Employee Training Dollars

Companies spend millions every year training their employees. Are they seeing results? This list provides a few concrete ways for making sure you get the most return for your training dollar.

1. Define a quantifiable organizational result - For example, use an objective like making more widgets for less or improving productivity by 5 percent.

2. Translate that into specific individual learning competencies - Make sure that the training goal is something an employee could learn (better procedures, new functions).

3. Determine industry standard best practices - Ask yourself: what would someone learn to help them develop these competencies?

4. Decide which employees should be trained - Some employees are likely to have or develop necessary practices, or are more critical to the goal.

5. Create a training program to help employees acquire these best practices - Consider using both internal or outsourced providers.

6. Establish an assessment system - Make sure the practices are being taught and that the learning is being applied toward meeting the goal.

The Larta Institute (www.larta.org)—an independent, private nonprofit corporation, originally formed in 1993.

Larta Institute manages programs that help companies innovate and grow. Their services include: Commercialization and Technology Transfer Conferences, Business Training, Consulting and Capital, Industry Research and Analysis Contact them at 714 West Olympic Boulevard, Suite 750, Los Angeles, CA 90015, phone: (213) 744-1314, email: mail@larta.org

9 Ways Outsourcing Your Manufacturing Can Improve Your Business

As companies consider whether to outsource manufacturing, it is important to break down the benefits and consider all impacts. In this list, discover the nine reasons companies should consider outsourcing their manufacturing.

1. More time to focus on core competency

By outsourcing manufacturing, a company no longer needs all the resources it has been using to make a product, store it and get it to the customer. The company can redirect these resources to its core functions. Workers will not be spread too thinly, managers will have time to focus more on processes, and leaders can concentrate on new ideas.

2. Reduce cost of manufacturing and logistics services

Consolidate operations by no longer maintaining factories, distribution centers (DCs) or inventory. The manufacturing and logistics costs to outsourced companies are lower because they are no longer responsible for physical plants and personnel related to these operations functions. In addition, the vendor might provide a shared service, so the company is not paying for underutilized capacity, which will lower inventory carrying costs.

3. Reduce head count of hourly workers and management

Outsourcing operations is one of the most effective methods to reduce head count. Instead of reducing head count with a mandate that each department cut 2.5 employees while keeping workload constant (or in many cases, increasing it), an entire department is cut along with the workload. This creates a department that will maintain and grow a company's core competencies without losing valuable personnel or taking on more responsibilities due to increased workload.

4. Improve accuracy

When someone only has to perform one task, it is likely that if that task involves a count or payouts, then the completed task will be more accurate. If the only thing to do is inventory, then the inventory count is more likely to be more accurate than if you need to supervise several plants, pay department bills and maintain a global network of DCs.

5. Flexibility and wider range of service

If you think focusing on a core competency and outsourcing the rest is limiting your company, you might want to think again. If you outsource non-core functions—be they primary or secondary—your company has no limits. You can offer your customers more because, although the company may actually be doing less within its four physical walls, it is accomplishing much more. You can increase production, ship greater amounts, and break into product lines heretofore not considered because everything is not being done in-house.

6. Access global networks and superior technology

During the years of the e-business boom, software vendors began linking carriers, suppliers and purchasers in collaborative networks that have continued to grow even after the dot-com bust. Using outsourcers means a company does not have to build complex networks on its own. Smaller operations can share space, as well as IT support and operations. All companies can leverage provider networks to consolidate loads.

7. Improve service

Outsource manufacturing improves service by shortening cycle times and speeding time to market. Tapping into capabilities not available internally increases scheduling flexibility and resource availability, which usually results in reduced time to market. Third party logistics providers (3PLs) receive and store raw material or finished inventory, consume inventory in the production process, produce finished goods, and ship finished goods to customers—all while maintaining inventory. So, improved inventory visibility and accountability, as well as on-time delivery, are all part of their packages. This ensures higher levels of customer satisfaction.

8. Improve quality
Many companies that have already outsourced manufacturing originally did so to cut costs. However, they have now found that not only can outsourcing reduce overhead, it can also improve quality. This quality improvement is due to the fact that outsourcing providers running volume operations have better quality assurance (QA) programs in place than the average company that is still trying to do it in-house. The results include fewer damages, less rework, improved response time to inquiries, and greater inventory accuracy.

9. Reduce capital investment and increase cash inflow
Outsourcing manufacturing will reduce capital investment because once it is contracted out, the facilities previously used by the company can be removed from the balance sheet. If you no longer make or assemble your product, then you no longer need to maintain factories. This makes capital funds more available for a company's core functions. Outsourcing can also eliminate the need to demonstrate return on equity from capital investments in non-core areas, and this can improve certain financial measurements. Companies can also sell equipment, facilities and licenses used in current operations and end up with an infusion of cash.

Dr. James A. Tompkins is an international authority on supply chain strategy, focusing on implementation of end-to-end supply chains that are demand driven. He has written or contributed to more than 30 books. He can be reached at www.tompkinsinc.com.

4 Outsourcing Mistakes To Avoid

Most small business owners outsource tasks. It makes sense nowadays, with the cost of employment so high, demand slow and the proliferation of qualified people around the world willing to undertake tasks at a reasonable price. And there are a bunch of great services, like Elance, oDesk and Guru that I've used to help me locate and hire professionals for specific tasks.

Recently, I hired Jeff, a technical programmer and database expert, through one of these sites to help us with a database project. In the end things turned out fine. But the job could've been a lot easier (and profitable) if I had done a better job managing him. Instead, I suffered headaches, delays and too many difficult conversations with my client. The problems weren't Jeff's fault. They were mine. I made at least four mistakes.

Mistake #1 – I outsourced a critical task to him. A significant part of this project was importing data from the client's old system into the new one we implemented. It was very important that all of their data migrated to the new system and this task alone took up the most hours of any of the other budgeted tasks. Handing this off to an untested outsourced person who I just met online, particularly when I knew that a failure could cost us the project, was a mistake. In the end, Jeff did accomplish what needed to be done. But there were many rocky episodes and a couple of moments when I was concerned whether it would be done at all. I put too much reliance on someone I barely knew and it was almost catastrophic. Never again will I use an outsourced person who is not under my complete control to accomplish a critical task, at least until I really get to know him.

Mistake #2 – I didn't supervise him enough. I assumed that Jeff, being a professional programmer and database expert, could undertake the job with my minimal involvement. Jeff was smart. And experienced. But he was also human. He can't read my mind. He had to make certain decisions on his own without my input. And some of them were different than what I wanted. So we had to do work over and fix mistakes. These are things that wouldn't have happened if I had treated Jeff like I treat my employees and kept a closer eye on what he was doing.

Mistake #3 – I assumed absolute dedication. In my ignorance I assumed that Jeff would be doing and thinking about nothing else other than my project during course of our relationship. But Jeff, like most independent professionals, had other clients to tend to as well. And this wasn't unreasonable – it's not as if I was paying him enough to absolutely sustain himself with my work alone. So there were times when my project had to take a back seat to others on his plate. And there were times when I couldn't reach Jeff because he was meeting with other clients. Next time, I need to build this into my relationship and work out a better communication schedule so that even if Jeff doesn't prioritize me all the time, I can still be assured that tasks are being completed on time.

Mistake #4 – I didn't make enough use of technology to help me. Things would've gone much smoother with our project if I had made use of some of the great (and really inexpensive) web based tools that are available to help manage remote workers and projects. Like Basecamp for project management. And Google Docs for collaboration. And Skype or FreeConferenceCall for communicating. For the most part I let Jeff update me through emails and spreadsheets. As a result, information was delayed and unshareable amongst others on the project. I won't make this mistake next time.

The good news is that the project's done and in the end things turned out well. Luckily, our client was reasonable and the people were good to work with. They understood that sometimes projects don't go as smooth as we'd like. And we're planning more work together. I'll continue to use Jeff. At least we've got some experience together under our belts. And I've certainly learned from my mistakes too. Managing an outsourced person is not as easy as people think.

Gene Marks runs a ten person technology consulting firm in Bala Cynwyd, PA. He can be reached at www.marksgroup.net

4 Tips And Resources For Managing Your Outsourced Contracting Manufacturing Relationships

To be successful in outsourcing manufacturing or design, engineering, sourcing, manufacturing, operations, document control and quality need to function in concert with your partner. From initial product specification to final sign-off, your product team must be in close contact with your outsourcing manufacturing partners to ensure that your cost, quality and schedule goals are met. While exchanging information with your manufacturing partners can be difficult, the following tips offer support on how to make it a success.

Tip 1: Enable manufacturing outsourcing collaboration
It is important to establish a collaborative relationship with your suppliers, contract manufacturers (CMs) and design partners from the start. By building a strong alliance it will be easier to tackle any challenges that arise during the design or manufacturing stages. Creating a process to submit feedback or other suggestions (like manufacturing change orders) enables communication to take place and strengthens collaboration between all parties.

Tip 2: Make it easy to share product data with outsourced manufacturers
Consider how best to share information with your partners. Many companies exchange product data with their partners via email or fax. But how can you be certain your partner obtains only the information that is pertinent to them? Plus, these methods can become laborious to manage as your product line changes and grows or you change suppliers. A

cloud-based solution to help manage product data and changes may be the solution for you — one that can help streamline the process and also provide secure access rights.

Tip 3: Support closed-loop design and sourcing processes
Selecting the right manufacturing firm for your business may mean working with a partner that is onshore or offshore. But regardless of your partners' location, establishing a way to capture improvement suggestions from your outsourced manufacturers that allows all product team members to stay in the loop can help to manage the impacts of a design change efficiently.

Tip 4: Drive active outsourced manufacturing participation
It can be challenging to keep all parties involved—especially if groups are geographically dispersed. Provide a framework for effective collaboration to get everyone on the same page. An infrastructure that allows all parties access to product data (i.e. bills of materials, engineering changes, etc.) can help drive contributions and keep everyone focused on the projects at hand.

*As vice president of product management and strategy, **Steve Chalgren** is responsible for setting product strategy, charting the product roadmap and leading the Arena product team (www.arenasolutions.com).*

8 Most Common Federal Labor Laws Every Manufacturer Should Know

As a business owner or manager, you may be unaware of the many labor laws out there. The following are a few of the most common federal labor laws you should know from the U.S. Department of Labor.

1. Fair Labor Standards Act (FLSA) - The Department of Labor enforces the *Fair Labor Standards Act (FLSA)*, which sets basic minimum wage and overtime pay standards. These standards are enforced by the Department's *Wage and Hour Division*, a program of the *Employment Standards Administration*. Workers who are covered by the FLSA are entitled to a *minimum wage*. Overtime pay at a rate of not less than one and one-half times their regular rate of pay is required after 40 hours of work in a workweek. Certain exemptions apply to specific types of businesses or specific types of work. The FLSA does not, however, require *severance pay*, *sick leave*, *vacations*, or *holidays*.

2. Davis-Bacon and Related Acts - The Davis-Bacon and Related Acts, which require payment of prevailing wage rates and fringe benefits on federally-financed or assisted construction.

3. Service Contract Act - The Service Contract Act, which requires payment of prevailing wage rates and fringe benefits on contracts to provide services to the federal government.

4. Contract Work Hours and Safety Standards Act - The Contract Work Hours and Safety Standards Act, which sets overtime standards for most federal service contracts, federally funded construction contracts, and federal supply contracts over $100,000.

5. Walsh-Healey Public Contracts Act - The Walsh-Healey Public Contracts Act, which requires payment of minimum wage rates and overtime pay on federal contracts to manufacture or provide goods to the federal government.

6. Family and Medical Leave Act (FMLA) - The *Family and Medical Leave Act (FMLA)* provides for up to 12 weeks of unpaid leave for certain medical and family situations (e.g., adoption) for either the employee or a member of the covered and eligible employee's immediate family; however, in many instances paid leave may be substituted for unpaid FMLA leave.

7. Immigration and Nationality Act of 1990 - The *Immigration and Nationality Act of 1990* applies to employers seeking to hire nonimmigrant aliens as workers in specialty occupations under H-1B visas.

8. Employee Retirement Income Security Act (ERISA) - Most private sector health plans are covered by the *Employee Retirement Income Security Act (ERISA)*. Among other things, ERISA provides protections for participants and beneficiaries in employee benefit plans (*participant rights*), including providing access to *plan information.* Also, those individuals who manage plans (and other fiduciaries) must meet certain standards of conduct under the fiduciary responsibilities specified in the law.

U.S. Department of Labor (www.dol.gov)—Frances Perkins Building, 200 Constitution Avenue, NW, Washington, DC 20210 1-(866)-4-USA-DOL, TTY: 1-(877)-889-5627.

12 Employee Notices You May Need To Post In Your Plant

Some federal and state agencies require that you post certain posters in the workplace where workers can see them. Typically, such posters are designed to inform workers about safety procedures, wage and hour laws and other statutes and regulations. Are you required to hang this information?

1. Fair Labor Standards Act (FLSA) - Every employer of employees subject to the Fair Labor Standards Act's minimum wage provisions must post, and keep posted, a notice explaining the Act in a conspicuous place in all of their establishments so as to permit employees to readily read it. The content of the notice is prescribed by the Wage and Hour Division of the Department of Labor.

2. Job Safety & Health Protection - All covered employers are required to display and keep displayed, a poster prepared by the Department of Labor* informing employees of the protections of the *Occupational Safety and Health Act* P.L. 91-596, December 29, 1970 and its amendments.

3. Family and Medical Leave Act (FMLA) - All covered employers are required to display and keep displayed a poster prepared by the Department of Labor summarizing the major provisions of The Family and Medical Leave Act (FMLA) and telling employees how to file a complaint. The poster must be displayed in a conspicuous place where employees and applicants for employment can see it. A poster must be displayed at all locations even if there are no eligible employees.

4. Equal Employment Opportunity Act - Every employer covered by the non-discrimination and EEO laws is required to post on its premises the poster, "Equal Employment Opportunity is the Law." The notice must be posted prominently, where it can be readily seen by employees and applicants for employment. The notice provides information concerning the laws and procedures for filing complaints of violations of the laws with the Office of Federal Contract Compliance Programs (OFCCP).

5. Migrant and Seasonal Agricultural Worker Protection Act (MSPA) - Each farm labor contractor, agricultural employer and agricultural association which is subject to the MSPA and who employs any migrant or seasonal agricultural worker(s) shall post and keep posted in a conspicuous place at the place of employment a poster prepared by the Department of Labor which explains the rights and protections for workers required under the Migrant and Seasonal Agricultural Worker Protection Act.

6. Notice To Workers With Disabilities - Each farm labor contractor, agricultural employer and agricultural association which is subject to the MSPA and who employs any migrant or seasonal agricultural worker(s) shall post and keep posted in a conspicuous place at the place of employment a poster prepared by the Department of Labor which explains the rights and protections for workers required under the Migrant and Seasonal Agricultural Worker Protection Act.

7. Employee Polygraph Protection Act (EPPA) - Every employer subject to the Employee Polygraph Protection Act (EPPA) shall post and keep posted on its premises a notice explaining the Act, as prescribed by the Secretary of Labor. Such notice must be posted in a prominent and conspicuous place in every establishment of the employer where it can readily be observed by employees and applicants for employment.

8. Uniformed Services Employment and Reemployment Rights Act (USERRA) - Employers are required to provide to persons entitled to the rights and benefits under the Uniformed Services Employment and Reemployment Rights Act (USERRA), a notice of the rights, benefits and obligations of such persons and such employers under USERRA. Employers may provide the notice, "Your Rights Under USERRA", by posting it where employee notices are customarily placed. However, employers are free to provide the notice to employees in other ways that will minimize costs while ensuring that the full text of the notice is provided (e.g., by handing or mailing out the notice, or distributing the notice via electronic mail).

9. The Davis Bacon Act - Every employer performing work covered by the labor standards of The Davis-Bacon and Related Acts shall post a notice (including any applicable wage determination) at the site of the work in a prominent and accessible place where it may be easily seen by employees.

10. The Beck Poster - Executive Order 13201 (E.O. 13201) requires Government contracts and subcontracts to include an employee notice clause requiring non-exempt Federal contractors and subcontractors to post notices informing their employees that they have certain rights related to union membership and use of union dues and fees under Federal law.

11. The Service Contract Act (SCA) - Every employer performing work covered by the Walsh-Healey Public Contracts Act or the McNamara-O'Hara Service Contract Act (SCA) is required to post a notice of the compensation required (including, for service contracts, any applicable wage determination) in a prominent and accessible location at the worksite where it may be seen by all employees performing on the contract.

12. Equal Employment Opportunity - Every employer covered by the non-discrimination and EEO laws is required to post on its premises the poster, "Equal Employment Opportunity is the Law." The notice must be posted prominently, where it can be readily seen by employees and applicants for employment. The notice provides information concerning the laws and procedures for filing complaints of violations of the laws with the Office of Federal Contract Compliance Programs (OFCCP).

Business.gov is a collaborative effort managed by the U.S. Small Business Administration. Partner executive departments include Department of Commerce (DOC)

Department of Labor, *Office of small business programs. www.dol.gov/osbp/sbrefa/poster/main.htm*

10 Great Manufacturing Compensation Strategies

Attracting the best talent isn't enough. Hiring and keeping top performers can improve individual and team productivity, boost morale, and grow profits. Here's a list of the most popular compensation strategies employed by today's top business managers. Some are obvious, though too many go overlooked.

1. Top-Market Salary.
While most pundits are projecting a 3% average salary increase in 2013, they also say high performers will continue to earn more. Why? Tight-fisted managers are giving way to a new breed that are paying top dollar for talent on the theory that outstanding performers will earn market rates anyway, and paying them top dollar reduces incentives to shop their talents. Be prepared to pay a little more from the outset.

2. Voluntary Equity Participation.
Historically, startups and big businesses alike have taken to offering equity as a salary substitute in hopes of improving cash flow while giving employees a long-term incentive to strive for. But that's changing. Now, some companies are giving workers a pot of cash to have either as salary or equity. Expand your definition of "compensation" to give workers more control.

3. Incentive Pay.
Otherwise known as performance pay, incentives are paid when measurable targets are met. They also carry a great deal of flexibility. Small businesses can choose to pay incentives only when the entire company meets a goal.

Others may incentivize teams or individual employees, or a combination of all three. However you design it, ensure incentives are only paid for performance that exceeds expected norms.

4. Insurance Coverage.
An increasingly elusive benefit in recent years thanks to cutbacks at small and large businesses. Meanwhile, in the U.S., federal rules are poised to leave millions without access to subsidies to help the uninsured pay for health care. Consider keeping coverage but include a sliding scale wherein the company covers premiums for the lowest paid workers while top earners pay their own way.

5. Matching Retirement Contributions.
Cash-strapped companies aren't matching retirement contributions as much as they used to. Most aren't giving up on the practice, however, choosing instead to stagger payments to qualified plans such as 401k and 403b accounts.

6. Unlimited Vacation.
An increasingly popular option thanks to new research that finds rested employees are more productive. For example, consulting firm Ernst & Young found that staff that took 10 additional hours of vacation each year earned higher performance scores from their supervisors. They were also less likely to leave for another job, the firm found. Give workers the time to recuperate and they'll reward you with better results.

7. Flexible Schedule.
Becoming more common thanks to advances in technology. Studies show that employees are 55% more engaged with work when operating with a flexible schedule. They've also been found to be 27% more productive.

8. Training and Tuition Reimbursement.
Typically available at larger companies, employers pay a percentage of tuition costs for some sort of job-related advanced education, certificate, seminar series or the like. As

with insurance coverage, consider a sliding scale where reimbursement is conditioned on class performance and job relevancy.

9. Job Portability.
While it's impossible to make tangible promises of growth in a compensation package, your culture should allow for employees who learn on the job to stretch and try new roles. Teach employees that there's room to grow and they'll be less likely to look elsewhere when seeking to advance their careers.

10. A Formal Recognition Program.
Most importantly, compensation must include never letting employees believe they aren't valued. Adopt a formal recognition program for rewarding successes small and large. Appreciation lunches. Cards. Even a personal visit from the CEO. Take explicit steps to recognize outstanding performance and you'll outperform peers that don't, according to research compiled by the Society For Human Resource Management.

*John Mills is executive vice president of Business Development at Rideau Recognition Solutions (*rideau.com*), a global leader in employee rewards and recognition programs designed to motivate and increase engagement and productivity across the workforce.*

10 Rules For Determining Overtime Pay In Your Shop

New federal regulations governing when employees are entitled to overtime pay took effect on August 23, 2004. The regulations were issued under the Fair Labor Standards Act (FLSA). The following are the rules for determining overtime pay.

1. Exempt vs. non-exempt

Under FLSA, unless exempt, employees must receive at least the federal minimum wage for all hours worked and overtime pay at 1½ times the regular rate of pay for all hours worked over 40 in a workweek. One of the most significant changes is the mandate that employers pay overtime to employees earning less than $455 a week or $23,660 annually. Under the prior law, employers had to pay overtime to employees earning less than $155 per week or $8,060 annually. The new regulations also replace the prior regulations' use of so-called "long" and "short" duties tests with new "standard" tests to ascertain if employees who earn between $23,660 and $100,000 annually are exempt from overtime payment requirements. The new regulations also create a new exemption from overtime payment requirements for certain "highly paid" employees who earn at least $100,000 a year. The new regulations also guarantee non-exempt status to employees in many "blue collar" occupations, removing any doubt about their eligibility for overtime pay.

2. White collar exemptions

The new regulations continue to provide an exemption from overtime payment requirements for bona fide executive, professional and administrative employees; outside salespersons; and certain computer professionals. However, many of the tests for exemptions have changed. The new tests are set out below, with a comparison to the prior regulations.

3. Executive exemption standard test
Under the new regulations, the executive employee exemption applies if:
1. The employee is compensated on a salary basis of at least $455 per week;
2. The employee's primary duty is to manage the enterprise or a customarily recognized department or subdivision of the enterprise;
3. The employee customarily and regularly directs the work of at least two or more other full-time employees or their equivalent; and
4. the employee has the authority to hire or fire other employees, or his suggestions and recommendations as to hiring, firing, advancement, promotion or any other change of status of other employees are given particular weight.

4. Administrative exemption standard test
Under the new regulations, the administrative employee exemption applies if:
1. The employee is compensated on a salary or fee basis of at least $455 a week;
2. The employee's primary duty consists of performing office or non- manual work directly related to the management or general business operations of the employer or the employer's customers; and
3. The employee's primary duty includes the exercise of of significance.

5. Professional exemption standard test
Under the new regulations, the learned professional employee exemption applies if:
1.The employee is paid on a salary or fee basis of at least $455 a week;

2. The employee's primary duty consists of performing work requiring advanced knowledge defined as work that is predominantly intellectual in character and that includes work requiring the consistent exercise of discretion and judgment;
3. The advanced knowledge is in a field of science or learning; and
4. Such advanced knowledge is customarily acquired by a prolonged course of specialized intellectual instruction.

Under the new regulations, to qualify for the creative professional employee exemption:
1. The employee must be compensated on a salary or fee basis of at least $455 a week; and
discretion and independent judgment with respect to matters
2. The employee's primary duty must consist of performing work requiring invention, imagination or talent in a recognized field of artistic endeavor.

6. Computer employee exemption test
Under the new regulations, the computer employee exemption generally applies if:

1. The employee is compensated on a salary basis of at least $455 a week or at a pay rate of at least $27.63 an hour;

2. The employee is employed as a computer systems analyst, computer programmer, software engineer or other similarly skilled worker in the computer field; and

3. The employee's primary duty consists of either
    (a) the application of systems analysis techniques and procedures;
    (b) the design, development, documentation, analysis, creation, testing or modification of computer systems or programs;
    (c) the design, documentation, testing, creation or modification of computer programs related to machine operating systems; or

(d) a combination of the duties and skills set forth in (a) through (c). Prior FLSA regulations contained a similar exemption for computer professionals.

7. Outside salesperson exemption

The new regulations also continue to provide an exemption from overtime for outside salespersons. This exemption applies to:

1. An employee whose primary duty is making sales, or obtaining orders or contracts for services or for the use of facilities for which a consideration will be paid by the client or customer; and

2. Where the employee is customarily and regularly engaged away from the employer's place or places of business. Besides the above requirements, the old regulations contained a confusing limitation on the amount of time an outside salesperson could spend performing non-exempt work. (Salespersons could perform non-exempt work during no more that 20 percent of the hours worked in the workweek by non-exempt employees of the employer.)

8. Highly compensated employee exemption

The new regulations include an added overtime exemption for "highly compensated employees" -- defined as employees who receive total annual compensation of $100,000 or more. These highly compensated employees are exempt only if they customarily and regularly perform at least one of the duties of an exempt executive, administrative employee or professional employee.

9. Blue collar workers

The new regulations reiterate that the exemptions from overtime only apply to white collar and not to manual laborers or other blue collar workers who perform work involving repetitive operations with their hands, physical skill and energy. Some of the FLSA-covered, non-management employees status -- are: carpenters, electricians, mechanics, plumbers, iron workers, craftsmen, operating engineers, longshoremen, construction workers and laborers. These employees are not exempt from overtime pay requirements even if they are highly paid.

10. First responders

The exemptions from overtime under the new regulations generally do not apply to "First Responders." First Responders include police officers, firefighters, paramedics, emergency medical personnel, rescue workers, hazardous materials workers and similar employees. These employees will not become exempt from overtime pay regardless of their pay level.

Charles H. Kaplan, Elizabeth A. Alcorn, David J. Weisenfeld, and Alice B. Stock from the New York office of Thelen Reid & Priest LLP. (www.thelenreid.com) Thelen Reid & Priest LLP is a national law firm with more than 440 attorneys. Information contained in this list should not be construed as legal advice or legal opinion, which can only be rendered when related to specific fact situations.

9 Key OSHA Requirements For Your Shop

Through its rulings, OSHA has developed a set of requirements that define its expectations of a comprehensive confined space protection program, including the proper use of confined space entry and retrieval equipment. OSHA standards may require that employers adopt certain practices, means, methods or processes reasonably necessary to protect workers on the job. It is the responsibility of employers to become familiar with standards applicable to their establishments, to eliminate hazardous conditions to the extent possible, and to comply with the standards Designed to provide workers with in-depth protection, these requirements include:

1. Access to Medical and Exposure Records
This standard requires that employers grant employees access to any of their medical records maintained by the employer and to any records the employer maintains on the employees' exposure to toxic substances.

2. Personal Protective Equipment
This standard, included separately in the standards for each industry segment (except agriculture), requires that employers provide employees, at no cost to employees, with personal protective equipment designed to protect them against certain hazards. This can range from protective helmets to prevent head injuries in construction and cargo handling work, to eye protection, hearing protection, hard-toed shoes, special goggles (for welders, for example) and gauntlets for iron workers.

3. Hazard Communication

This standard requires that manufacturers and importers of hazardous materials conduct a hazard evaluation of the products they manufacture or import. If the product is found to be hazardous under the terms of the standard, containers of the material must be appropriately labeled and the first shipment of the material to a new customer must be accompanied by a material safety data sheet (MSDS). Employers, using the MSDSs they receive, must train their employees to recognize and avoid the hazards the materials present.

4. Hazard-free workplace

In general, all employers (except those in the construction industry) should be aware that any hazard not covered by an industry-specific standard may be covered by a general industry standard; in addition, all employers must keep their workplaces free of recognized hazards that may cause death or serious physical harm to employees, even if OSHA does not have a specific standard or requirement addressing the hazard. This coverage becomes important in the enforcement aspects of OSHA's work.

5. Recordkeeping

Every employer covered by OSHA who has more than 10 employees, except for certain low-hazard industries such as retail, finance, insurance, real estate, and some service industries, must maintain OSHA-specified records of job-related injuries and illnesses. There are two such records, the OSHA Form 200 and the OSHA Form 101.

6. Reporting

In addition to the reporting requirements described above, each employer, regardless of number of employees or industry category, must report to the nearest OSHA office within 8 hours of any accident that results in one or more fatalities or hospitalization of three or more employees. Such accidents are often investigated by OSHA to determine what caused the accident and whether violations of standards contributed to the event.

7. Employees

Employees must be provided with jobs and a place of employment free from recognized hazards that are causing, or are likely to cause, death or serious physical harm. Do not discriminate against employees who exercise their rights under the OSH Act. Also provide well-maintained tools and equipment, including appropriate personal protective equipment to all employees. Provide medical examinations and training required by OSHA standards. Post prominently the OSHA poster (OSHA 3165) informing employees of their rights and responsibilities.

8. Accidents

Accidents that result in fatalities or that result in the hospitalization of three or more employees must be reported to OSHA within 8 hours. Keep records of work-related accidents, injuries, illnesses and their causes and post annual summaries for the required period of time. A number of specific industries in the retail, service, finance, insurance, and real estate sectors that are classified as low-hazard are exempt from most requirements of the regulation, as are small businesses with 10 or fewer employees (see 29 CFR Part 1904).

9. Notices

Post OSHA citations and abatement verification notices at or near the worksite. Abate cited violations within the prescribed period. Respond to survey requests for data from the Bureau of Labor Statistics, OSHA, or a designee of either agency.

Environmental Health & Safety Online, (www.ehso.com) is for EHS Professionals and the general public. They find credible public domain sources of research, such as public research institutions and government scientific websites; gather the key information from them; organize it, often re-

write it and publish it. EHSO is one place to easily find the best source of environmental, health and safety guidance. **Contact them at EHSO, Inc., 8400-O Roswell Rd., Atlanta, GA 30350 Tel: (770) 263-8700**

Chapter 4: Your Sales
And Marketing

5 Interview Questions Every Manufacturer Should Ask A Prospective Sales Manager

When hiring a sales manager into a manufacturing company, industry experience isn't as important as you think. You already have, internally, the expertise and knowledge about your industry that can be taught to a strong managerial candidate. That said, below are five questions hiring managers should ask more often, including some of the answers you'll want to hear from qualified candidates.

1. Is cold calling dead?
Some interviewees may get defensive, or think this is a trick question. The answer, of course, is no. When all else fails (market conditions, marketing leads, etc.), picking up the phone is the one thing sales reps will always be able to control. But how they cold call – who they call, with what message and offer, at what frequency and cadence – is extremely important. Cold calling must be customer-centric and value-driven to succeed in today's buyer-centric world.

2. Should reps get warm leads or build their own pipelines?
Similar question, different angle. The right answer is typically to get warm leads, but not because the reps are lazy or can't successfully build their own business from the ground up. Lead-driven sales are typically more cost effective than having expensive sales reps cold calling. Yes, leads are expensive up-front, but the eventual cost per acquisition and overall lifetime value and margin for the

business on those new customers is usually much better when reps are making more efficient use of their time with warm leads.

3. What's the ideal relationship between sales and marketing, and how do you operationalize that?
It's more than just inviting marketing to your meetings. The ideal relationship starts with common goals of what success looks like, common definitions of leads, qualified leads, lead stages and short-term opportunities. It's working together on the same pipeline, and ensuring that success is measured and compensation is dispensed based on overall pipeline performance. Marketing needs to be held accountable for qualified opportunities and closed business. When that alignment takes place, the daily and weekly operational requirements more easily fall into place.

4. Should sales reps be paid commission?
Yes, there are more companies today that put their reps on a salary. But the best reps still want the variability of compensation, because they want the upside. They will happily take the risk (and the occasional bad month or quarter) to earn a C-level paycheck when they hit it out of the park.

5. Why don't you want to make more money as an individual contributor?
Great question to ask prospective sales managers. The right answer comes down to how many commission checks they want. Sales managers will still have a portion of their compensation come as a performance bonus or commission based on their team's performance. The best sales managers know they can make far more money as a manager in these conditions, buy not just driving higher sales themselves but improving the performance and consistently higher sales of an entire team. Sales managers still want their money, but they know the upside is actually higher as a manager with a good comp plan.

Matt Heinz is a must follow B2B marketer according to optify.net, and president of Heinz Marketing (www.heinzmarketing.com), a Redmond-based sales & marketing firm. You can connect with Matt via email (matt@heinzmarketing.com), Twitter (@heinzmarketing), LinkedIn (www.linkedin.com/in/mattheinz) or his blog (www.heinzmarketing.com/matt-on-marketing/blog/).

6 Things You Should Expect From A Manufacturer's Rep

At a minimum, you should expect your rep to **understand their products and services**. But there's more.

1. **An update on the company** — What has been its successes and its shortcomings. If you have "hitched your wagon" to a company, then you need to know we are headed in the right direction, bringing new, innovative products to market, adding staff to accommodate growth, and improving the overall customer service experience for you, the distributor, and ultimately for your customer. I always try to give a little State of the Union in my meetings. You need to have confidence in us.

2. **Industry knowledge.** I never talk about a specific customer and their methods, but I might tell you that "many companies are having great success with venue-based marketing" or that there are a lot of customers doing well with Sacagawea. We want to give you information that will help direct your company.

3. **Mentoring of new employees.** We aren't trying to run your company, but many times a new employee just needs to talk to a veteran. It may be about strategies or products or industry history or specific venues. I get asked tons of travel-related questions because I have done so much of it. I look at mentoring as another way to offer advice and make friends.

4. "Grease the wheel" from time to time. When you are struggling with something, and it isn't making sense and adding up, call your manufacturer's rep to ask them to get involved. We can sometimes prevent issues from developing (if you see problems coming). We also can get far deeper into "the system" than you, the customer can. Think of us is as your rep.

5. Be a listener. The customer always needs to feel comfortable in "venting" to you. Sometimes they just need to be heard. The last thing you ever want is for your clients to think you don't care or are only giving lip service. Listen. Listen twice as much as you talk. That's why you have two ears and only one mouth

6. Be a friend, or at least a close colleague. Friends buy from friends. So if you really want to boil down everything to one simple thought: we are out to make friends. Can you become friends with your customers? Do you like people and are you genuinely interested in their lives. I have been to weddings, funerals, vacations, concerts, sporting events, fishing and hunting trips. They are all opportunities to engage and spend time with a customer and a friend. It makes my life richer because I like and respect them . . . and if it adds to our business growth, then that is a bonus. To build a better relationship, just be friends.

Reid Sherwood is a National Sales Manager with ClassicMODUL. Sherwood has built a solid reputation in the trade show industry with sales, marketing, and production experience. He can be reached at reid@classicmodul.com.

7 Top Considerations When Hiring A Manufacturers' Rep

Manufacturers' reps are not just experts on your product; they also are experts in their local market area. And, unlike a direct employee who may be looking for the bigger paycheck that comes with being promoted from the Omaha office to the Chicago office, your Omaha manufacturers' rep has roots in the community and has no desire to be "promoted" away from friends and family. Since his or her "inventory" is years or decades of experience in the Omaha market, why would he or she want to relocate and leave that behind?

1. Where do I find good reps?
To be sure you get to interview the best candidates for your line there are three key bases that must be covered: Existing customers, current reps and rep trade associations.

2. What are the advantages of manufacturers' reps?
Hiring reps instead of a direct sales force avoids all the fixed costs of direct sales employees: Salary, medical insurance, workers compensation, human resources, travel and entertainment, and more. If you have a relatively narrow product line, your rep can bundle your products with products from other manufacturers on his or her line card and include your product in a package deal you could not easily put together yourself.

3. What are the disadvantages of manufacturers' reps?
You can set a high sales bar for reps, and they will achieve it, but you generally can't tell them how to achieve it. Reps are independent businesspeople, and although they welcome

a challenge and stretch goals, most will want to set their own plans on how to achieve those goals rather than allowing a manufacturer to dictate how those goals should be achieved. If you tend to be a micromanager, you probably will not be successful with reps.

4. How do I get more of a rep's time?
It's surprisingly easy. It's really just basic blocking and tackling. Offer a quality product at a market-friendly price, ship the product on time, and pay the rep on time. This seems simple, but so many manufacturers lose track of blocking and tackling that if you do all the fundamentals well, you will be a stand-out on most reps' line cards, and you will do well.

5. Do I have to pay the rep commission on accounts I already had before I hired the rep?
Most reps expect to work hard to earn their commissions and understand that developing new accounts often involves investing their time into a long sales cycle. And they generally will use sales commissions for accounts that came with the territory to help finance those long-term efforts. Commissions on existing sales usually don't cover all the rep's costs to develop new customers, but they do help the rep offset some of those costs until sales commission on new accounts start. Keeping existing accounts as no-commission "house accounts" will get your new rep relationships off to a rocky start, and many reps will decline to accept a new line that has house accounts,

6. So, if I don't have any sales, reps will work for free?
Reps are in business to make a profit just like you are, so the results you can expect when you ask a rep to work "for free" probably will be disappointing. Reps who accept a "pioneering" line with no existing commissions can't afford to take time away from manufacturers who are already paying them commission, so their efforts may be limited to "Oh, by the way, we also have 'x' if you need it." If you need to hire a rep in a territory that has no existing sales, consider offering a monthly "territory development fee" or

stipend to help with the costs of territory development in exchange for monthly reports on those pioneering efforts.

7. Now that we've found the right rep, is a handshake good enough?

No. Many a rep/principal relationship has turned sour because years later each party remembers the particulars of a handshake agreement differently. Or perhaps either or both of the parties who made the handshake agreement leave the company or retire, leaving the remaining parties to try to reconstruct what might have happened years ago. Your corporate attorney is generally not the right person to write that agreement. Rep agreements are a legal specialty, just like income taxes, human resources, or trusts. Not-for-profit rep associations can recommend a rep-savvy attorney in your area, and MANA offers specimen contracts that you can use as a basis for conversation with the attorney who will ultimately write your agreement.

Charles M. Cohon is CEO and President of the Manufacturers' Agents National Association (MANA) www.manaonline.org. MANA is a not-for-profit trade association that brings reps and manufacturers together and helps them to develop the skills and tools they need to become professional partners in profit. Cohon brings two decades of experience as the founder of an extremely successful electrical rep company to his role with MANA. He earned an MBA with honors from the University of Chicago Booth School Of Business and is a speaker and author on a variety of aspects of sales force outsourcing.

5 Ways Manufacturers Can Increase Sales

There are proactive ways to increase your sales right now – this year. Here are five.

1. Get specified basis-of-design more often!

If a manufacturer is the basis of design on an engineer's project, they have a 65%+ chance of being selected on the project. Why? Because it is easier for the contractor to get the engineer to approve it. They are providing what the engineer and Owner want for the job. If the contractor picks another manufacturer's product, then they may be partially "on the hook" if there are problems. You must have a program to have your products listed by manufacturer in all the consulting engineer's master specifications.

2. Make it faster and easier for your reps to quote jobs

Manufacturers must understand their sales reps are making decisions every hour of every day on what they spend their time on to earn their living. If you were a sale rep under tremendous time pressure, and Manufacturer A takes 1 hour to quote a job, and Manufacturer B takes 5 minutes to quote the same job, which manufacturer's price do you think will bid the job? It is absolutely imperative to have a pricing and quoting system that is designed to give reps quick ball park pricing as well as detailed pricing to meet the workflows that reps do every day. Keep it simple, fast, and no barriers to create a job, enter the options, and get quick prices and quotes.

3. Track your sales reps quote/order activity

To increase sales, it is critical to have the best sales rep force you can get in all the sales territories. To understand if a sales rep performance, you must track metrics and compare to other territories. Most manufacturers know the orders/sales by rep office, but they have no idea which reps are quoting, what they are quoting and why they are losing jobs? Keep track of these metrics:

A) the total number and value of quotes per month.
B) Rep office quote to order ratio. Compare rep offices by the ratio. High ratios means there is some reason they are not closing deals, like high multipliers, or not basis of design. Low quotes means they are not spending time quoting or your products are not specified.

4. Let the world know why they should buy your product rather than competitors

Customer service and support is huge for your customers. If you are good at it, then let them know it. Remind them of it. For important projects, they need good customer service. What is your competitive edge over your competitors? Is it price? Better performance? Higher efficiency? Customer service? Faster lead times? I find so much marketing material that does not list this essential information. This needs to be the elevator pitch – in 10 seconds or less, why should I consider buying you over the next guy? And it needs to be crystal clear to your customers and consulting engineers. Make sure all your sales staff, reps, distributors, and customers know why they should buy from you rather than your competitors. If you are not sure, ask your rep force "Why do you like buying our product from us?" You will be amazed at the answers you will receive.

5. Go after a few big fish this year

Target a big market like a large national account, a large metropolitan city, federal government, or selling to a new country that can add a significant amount to the bottom line. Put someone in charge of focusing on researching big fish and landing that business. Give them a target sales number and see what they come up with. If you got on board with the largest rep firm handling New York City, what would that mean to your bottom line?

Brian Cumming, PE is a veteran consulting engineer, former owner of a successful MEP consulting engineering firm, and owner of BCA Technologies. He has helped many HVAC manufacturers increase their sales using the latest software technologies. Connect with Brian at brianc@bcatech.com.

7 More Ways Manufacturing Companies Can Increase Sales

Many of today's manufacturers are facing significant challenges in utilizing the Internet to increase sales. So what are some things that make a difference?

1. Invest in a great design. Image matters. Companies that make great products need to present a strong image and the corporate web site is the place to do it. A great image can make the difference in lost or closed sales when prospective customers are performing the "sniff test" on your company to see if you can deliver.

2. Present your catalog online. I'm not just talking about a PDF download. I'm talking about having a full-fledged interactive product catalog that allows your customers to search, browse, and research your products online. Products should not simply be listed on a page, but should be part of a true product database so that individual product listings can be sent to prospective customers electronically as a link or via social media. This speeds up the sales cycle and gives your sales team better support as they present products. If possible, include video demos.

3. Collect leads. Manufacturing websites should be asking site visitors for names and email addresses so that email communications on new and updated products can be delivered. This keeps prospective customers in your funnel and improves your chances of reaching them when it comes time to buy.

4. Facilitate an ecosystem. Manufacturing companies can benefit a great deal from creating online communities that their customers can use to communicate with each other and share knowledge. This helps build value around your company's brand and improves retention. An ecosystem can be an online forum, an extranet, or even a Facebook Group.

5. Utilize search engine optimization (SEO). Most manufacturing companies are not investing very heavily in SEO campaigns. This opens up a huge opportunity for those who do. By investing in targeted search engine marketing, smart manufacturing companies can ensure that their products show up at the top of the list when prospective customers are doing research online. This can make the difference between lost business or closed business.

6. Distribute documentation. If your products come with documentation that helps your customers better understand how to use or implement your products, post it on your website - all of it. By driving your customers back to your website, you are reinforcing the value of your brand. It also allows you to eliminate or reduce printed documentation, which saves money. Online documentation can also be updated in minutes - a huge advantage over printed documentation. I'm not referring to PDF downloads, I'm referring to an online database of documentation that your customers can search and sort easily to find what they need. This makes you easy to do business with and improves retention. It's also a great sales tool because prospective customers can see how easy it is to get the supporting information they need about your products which reduces anxiety.

7. Increase your PR efforts using Social Media. Manufacturing companies should be investing in PR to increase brand awareness and tell a story. Social Media is a great way to extend your PR efforts. Press releases should be listed on your company website and then distributed via Twitter, Facebook, and LinkedIn. This improves your search

124

engine rankings and encourages others to re-distribute your content for you. Make sure your website content includes "share this" buttons to facilitate easy distribution by site visitors. Many manufacturing companies are not taking full advantage of their company websites to leap ahead of the competition which means that the ones who do will have a significant advantage. Support your sales team and your customers with a great website and enjoy greater customer loyalty and increased sales.

Michael Reynolds is President/CEO of SpinWeb (spinweb.net*), a digital agency located in Indianapolis, IN. As an Inbound Marketing Certified Professional with Honors Distinction, Michael regularly blogs, publishes educational industry content, and speaks at conferences around the country covering topics like social media strategies, inbound marketing, and technology.*

3 Ways Manufacturers Can Use Social Media To Win Business

As global manufacturers increase their social media spending, the case for small- to mid-sized manufacturers to invest in social media grows stronger. The opportunities are particularly attractive in the contract and job shop manufacturing segments, which have traditionally relied on word-of-mouth marketing to win new business. I'd like to share three ways that manufacturers can start using social media today to improve their brand visibility and win more business.

1. Create a Blog to Tell Your Story
Blogs give manufacturers an opportunity to do more than just promote their brand. Blogs allow manufacturers to communicate with their customers and prospects using a richer form of media with longer-form stories. They're also a great avenue for sharing company information and providing industry knowledge. Manufacturers can use blogs to announce major company milestones, such as getting ISO 9001 certification, as well as share general industry trends and news. By striking a balance between promoting a brand and sharing useful information, manufacturers can gain a thought leadership position that will help win customers later down the road.

2. Start a YouTube Channel to Enrich Content
YouTube can be a great tool that educates buyers while subtly marketing through video. With the dramatically decreased cost of video production, creating a decent quality video is affordable and relatively easy today. Manufactures

should consider creating a YouTube video that provides a demonstration of products and processes, a tour of the factory, or showcases customer testimonials. Of course, the challenge is sticking to a video format that customers find relevant and engaging.

3. Use LinkedIn to Help Fill the Sales Funnel

A final tool that I'd like to highlight here is LinkedIn. For manufacturers, getting the most out of LinkedIn requires more than just becoming a member of the social network. Manufacturers can use LinkedIn to prime to sales funnel by using their networks to gain access to sales prospects. Once you get a few hundred contacts, your typical network usually reaches in the millions. This network can be used to get an introduction to a potential sales contact – or at the very least to connect with someone that can help strategize on how to contact the prospect. LinkedIn can also be a great place to demonstrate industry expertise by participating in relevant community discussions. Answering a difficult question in a Q&A forum, for instance, could very well lead to an unexpected contract.

Derek Singleton graduated from Occidental College in Los Angeles, CA with a BA in Political Science. Shortly after graduating, he began writing for the Software Advice blog as an ERP Market Analyst. He covers the distribution, manufacturing and supply chain software markets with special attention paid to the business benefits of information technology. He particularly enjoys writing about the relevance of technology to sustainability and greening efforts. To reach him, email derek@softwareadvice.com.

5 Marketing Ideas Manufacturers Should Embrace And 5 To Avoid

Remember the old line about how half of all marketing dollars are wasted but no one knows which half? The truth is, the best marketers do know. The following two lists highlight what great marketers try awfully hard to avoid – and what they work awfully hard to do instead.

Five Worst Marketing Ideas

These marketing landmines masquerade as quick fixes. When the business chips are down, they pop up to look like good solutions, but don't be fooled. Instead, make sure every new marketing effort soars above every single idea on this list.

1. Fight bad business with good advertising. - Here's the scenario: Business is down, so the owner points fingers at the economy and the competition and decides to run ads to overcome the problem. But the economy and the competition likely aren't the only culprits. Business is down because customers have defected – and new prospects haven't been converted – because the company's product or service is lacking. Running ads before improving the offering will only put a spotlight on the problem. In the words of advertising legend Bill Bernbach, "Nothing kills a bad product like a good ad." So fix the product and polish the service, and then run the ad.

2. Save the best for last. - It happens in presentations, sales letters, and ads. Businesses wait to divulge the greatest benefits of their product until the last minute, thinking that prospects will be sitting on the edges of chairs in rapt anticipation. Not so. If your opening doesn't grab them, they won't wait around. Four out of five people read only the headline, most listen to only the first few seconds of a broadcast ad, and if the first impression of a personal presentation, email subject line or online communication is weak, they tune out for the rest. The remedy: Commit to eliminate slow starts and to lead with your strengths.

3. Change your logo often and dramatically. - And while you're at it, change your website constantly. And your advertising tagline, too. It sounds ridiculous, but it's what happens when businesses let media departments, freelance artists, employees, and others create materials without the strong parameters of image guidelines to ensure a consistent company image. If you want prospects to trust that yours is a strong, steady business (and you do!), commit to developing and presenting a strong, steady business image.

4. Build it and trust they will come. - Sorry, but consumers aren't just sitting around waiting for the next new business, new website, new branch outlet, or new event to come into existence. They need to be told, reminded, inspired and given reasons and incentives to take new buying actions. In other words, when you build it, build a plan to market it.

5. Believe your customer is captive. - Reality is, your customers know they have other options. If they're standing in front of you, and you turn your attention to answer a phone, they notice. If you offer new customers a better deal than current customers enjoy, they notice. If you spend more time and money courting new prospects than rewarding business from current clientele, they most certainly notice and in time will disengage from your business as a result. Protect your business by realizing that customer loyalty is the key to profitability, and that earning it, appreciating it, and rewarding it with thanks and favors is a never-ending process.

Five Best Marketing Ideas

One marketing idea towers above all the others: *Write, commit to, and invest wisely in a marketing plan for your business.* Then as you implement your marketing program, join the best marketers by embracing the following ten ideas.

1. Make a great product before you make a great ad. - Be prepared before you promote. Be sure your product is ready for prime time before you announce its availability. Be sure you have an adequate inventory to fulfill the interest your marketing will generate. Be sure your distribution and sales channels are in place. Be sure your staff is knowledgeable about your product and about the ads you're running. And be sure that your is business is prepared to provide enthusiastic service that exceeds what customers might encounter at any competing business.

2. Sweat the big stuff. - Make a great first impression. Put at least as much effort into your ad headline as into your body copy. Devote at least as much energy to your introduction as to the entire rest of your sales presentation. Invest in your business lobby, the home page of your website, the cover of your brochure, the first sentence of a phone call, and every other first impression you're lucky enough to make for your business. People decide to tune in based on early snap judgments and if you don't grab them with a strong opening, they won't be around to hear the details.

3. Like your customers. - People buy from people they like, and from people who seem to genuinely like them in return. Treat every customer as an individual. Eliminate one-size-fits-all sales pitches. Listen to your customer's needs and tailor your communications in response. Make eye contact. Personalize online communications. Build rapport. Nurture interactions. Deliver value and continually enhance the customized service you train your customer to expect.

4. Increase value before lowering prices. - When customers see a price tag, they start a mental balancing act.

In a split second they perform some pretty elaborate mental calculations to determine whether the product under consideration is worth the price being asked. They weigh the price against their assessment of the quality, features, convenience, reliability, trustworthiness, guarantee of excellence, and ongoing service they believe they can count on as part of the deal. If they think the price exceeds the value of the product under consideration, you have two choices: ask for less money – or offer more value. Because prices can only go so low, and value can increase without limit, the best marketers know that enhancing value is the best first plan of attack.

5. Break down barriers. - Eliminate unnecessary expenses, unnecessary waits, unnecessary frustration, unnecessary inconvenience. Eliminate management layers that contribute costs without value. Eliminate service snags that cost time and try patience. Eliminate the reasons behind recurring problems. Eliminate inconveniences that stand between you and your customer. If your phone system is annoying, replace it. If your website is slow or crashes frequently, rebuild it. If getting to your business is inconvenient, take away the obstacles or find a way to bring your business to your customer via, mail, e-mail, e-commerce, or personal delivery. Eliminate anything that erodes the value for which your customer is willing to pay a premium.

Excerpted from books by **Barbara Findlay Schenck**, *author of Small Business Marketing Kit For Dummies, and* Selling Your Business For Dummies, *co-author of* Branding For Dummies *and* Business Plans Kit For Dummies, *and a syndicated marketing columnist and presenter. Follow her on Twitter @Bizstrong or visit www.bizstrong.com.*

8 Marketing Tips For Manufacturers

If there's one thing that no small business can live without, it's an effective marketing strategy. Your customers aren't going to find you without one, and without customers, you don't have a business. Here are eight simple tips for getting your company's name out there. How many are you currently utilizing?

1. Utilize Free Marketing Techniques
The first rule of small business marketing is to take full advantage of free marketing techniques. Your business should be signed up to all major social media websites. Your business should be active on all major social media accounts. Barter with neighboring businesses for advertising/customer referrals. Promote word of mouth marketing by over delivering for all customers.

2. Get Your Website in Order
Your website is available to customers 24 hours per day, 7 days per week. What exactly is it saying about your business? If you haven't already done so, invest in a high quality design and some top notch content. Next there's the small matter of traffic, the old "build it and they will come" adage is no longer true. If you want people to find you, you need to proactively attract them to your website. Look into both PPC advertising and SEO techniques.

3. Think About Starting a Blog
If your target demographic is even remotely internet savvy, think about starting a business blog. Here are a few tips:

- A business blog should be hosted on the same domain as your website.
- It must be updated on a regular basis.
- Posts should be relevant to both your business and its industry.
- Above all else, a business blog must be entertaining i.e. no sales pitches.

4. Reward Customer Loyalty

Multiple studies have shown that retaining an existing customer is five times cheaper than attracting a new one. In other words, promoting customer loyalty should be at the very top of your list of priorities. The easiest way to encourage repeat business is to simply offer discounts on future purchases. From a free cup of coffee for every six purchased, to a twenty percent discount on future purchases, this is a strategy that just about any business can implement.

5. Always be Networking

As a small business owner, you should be networking at every opportunity.

- Sign up to all relevant communities on LinkedIn.
- Never leave the house without business cards.
- Get involved in community charities/events.
- Ask your family and friends to spread the word about your business.

6. Seek Out Customer Testimonials

Seek out customer testimonials and publish them on your website and social media accounts. Collecting testimonials doesn't cost you a penny but they are highly effective when it comes to increasing a potential customers trust in your company. If you don't want to ask for testimonials directly, put up a sign asking your customers to rate your business on Yelp.com. It's also well worth including a link to your Yelp.com page on your website.

7. Start a Monthly Newsletter

Email marketing is well known for being one of the most cost effective marketing techniques. Obviously, the first thing that you are going to need is some email addresses. Ask your customers, social media followers and website visitors. Once you've built up a reasonably large database of willing recipients, start sending out a brief monthly newsletter that includes your latest products and promotions.

8. Know What Works

Finally, there's the small matter of tracking. It's essential for you to understand exactly where your customers are coming from. Otherwise how are you going to judge the cost effectiveness of your individual campaigns? Here are a few tips.

- Monitor your website and blog traffic. Is it a result of SEO or PPC?
- How often are people using your reward cards?
- Use different coupon codes for different marketing campaigns. Keep track of how often each one is used.
- Ask all customers, online and in store, how they found you.
- Switch things up occasionally and monitor the difference.

Writewell of the Berkeley Sourcing Group is well known for contract manufacturing in California. He makes sense when he says, that marketing is as important as the product itself for a business. A helpful guy, he gives useful advice to fellow businessmen on his blog.

7 Ways To Maximize Your Next Manufacturing Trade Show

Tradeshows can be very expensive. Sometimes it's worth the investment, many times it's not. Before attending a tradeshow, you must first decide why you will attend, then what you will do before, during and after the show. This will take some organization and time initially, however it will pay off in the long term. The following are some important benefits of attending tradeshows.

1. Conduct market research:
Tradeshows offer such a great variety of information. You will have the opportunity to sample products and services from hundreds of different vendors in a short amount of time.

2. Meet existing suppliers and customers:
It will depend on your business, but you can make weeks or months' worth of sales calls or meetings in a very short period of time.

3. Investigate new suppliers:
If you are not happy with your current supplier or products, this is the perfect opportunity to quickly and efficiently interview new companies.

4. Conduct business meetings:
You can meet colleagues and customers over coffee or after an educational session. To do this same thing without the show, it would cost you money and time.

5. Correct a problem:
If you have a problem with a current product, take this opportunity at the show to visit that supplier's exhibit and ask if they can help you solve the problem.

6. Network with colleagues:
If you cannot afford to be there as an exhibitor, being a delegate is the next best thing. It will give you the opportunity to be "seen" in the industry and remain "current".

7. Attend educational sessions:
Some trade shows offer break out seminars and lectures. Again, in just a few days you can obtain information that would take you months without the show.

GFTC - Guelph Food Technology Center (www.gftc.ca) - Canada's only not-for-profit, non-subsidized food technology centre. GFTC provides creative, confidential technical solutions, training, consulting and auditing to the Canadian agri-food industry in the areas of R&D, product development, packaging, shelf-life, food safety, quality, and productivity improvement. And they attend a lot of trade shows! Contact: 88 McGilvray Street, Guelph, Ontario, N1G 2W1, Canada, Tel. (519) 821-1246, Fax. (519) 836-1281, E-mail: gftc@gftc.ca

10 Tips For Using Tradeshow Giveaways Effectively

Walk around any trade or consumer show and you will be able to collect a bag full of advertising specialties, or giveaway items all designed to promote. But look a little more closely. When thinking about advertising specialties for your next show, consider the following ten questions:

1. What do you want to achieve by giving away a premium item?
Your giveaway items should be designed to increase your memorability, communicate, motivate, promote or increase recognition. It is important not only that the message have an impact, but also the premium itself.

2. How will you select your premium item?
There is a multitude of different items you could consider as a premium. However, which one will best suit your purpose? To select the right item, you need to decide your objective. Do you want it to enhance a theme; convey a specific message or educate your target audience? A clear purpose should help make your selection process easier. A promotional specialist can also help you make an effective selection. Remember that your company image is reflected in whatever you choose to give away.

3. Whom do you want to receive your premium?
Having a clear objective for your premium item will also help you decide who should receive it. You may consider having different gifts for different types of visitors. You

might have different quality gifts for your key customers, prospects and general passersby.

4. How does your giveaway tie into your marketing theme?

Is there an item that naturally complements your marketing message? Have the message imprinted on the item and make sure that your company name, logo and phone number appear clearly. An important aspect of any gift is to remember who it was from long after the fact.

5. What is your budget?

The price range for premium items is enormous. Quality, quantity and special orders, all impact the price. Establish a budget as part of your exhibit marketing plan. Consider ordering the same item for several different shows. The greater the quantity of your order, the lower the individual unit price.

6. What must visitors do to qualify for a gift item?

There are several ways to use your premium effectively. For example, as a reward for visitors participating in a demonstration, presentation or contest; as a token of your appreciation when visitors have given you qualifying information about their specific needs; as a thank you for stopping at the booth. Avoid leaving items out for anyone to take. This diminishes value and has little or no memorability factor.

7. Will your giveaway directly help your future sales?

Consider handing out a discount coupon or a gift certificate that requires future contact with your company for redemption. Consider premiums that will help generate frequent visits to customers and prospects, such as calling you for free refills.

8. How does your premium item complement your exhibiting goals?

Premiums can be used to prequalify your prospects. One company uses playing cards. Prior to the show, they send "kings" to their key customers, "queens" to suppliers, "jacks" to new or hot prospects. They request that the cards are brought to the booth in exchange for a special gift. When the cards are presented, the booth staff already know certain information about the visitor. They can then act on their previous knowledge and use time with the visitor more productively.

9. How will you inform your target audience about you giveaway item?

A sufficiently novel or useful giveaway can actively help to draw prospects to your booth. So make sure your prospects know about it. Send a "tickler" invitation with details of the giveaway, or create a two-piece premium, sending one part out to key prospects prior to the show and telling them to collect the other half at your booth.

10. How will you measure the effectiveness of your premium?

Establish a tracking mechanism to measure the success of your giveaway. If it is a redemption item, code it so that you know it resulted from the show. Post-show follow-up could include a question about the premium—did visitors remember receiving it and how useful was the item. After the show, critique your giveaway with your exhibit team: Did it draw specific prospects to the booth? Was it eye-catching enough to persuade passersby to stop? Did your customers find it useful? Did it project the right corporate image?

Susan Friedmann, CSP (Certified Speaking Professional), The Tradeshow Coach, Lake Placid, NY, author, "Meeting & Event Planning for Dummies," works with exhibitors, show organizers and meeting planners to create more valuable results from their events nationally and internationally. Website: www.thetradeshowcoach.com

10 Common Tradeshow Exhibiting Mistakes Manufacturers Make

We all make mistakes, however, if we are aware of the pitfalls that can occur, there is a better chance we can avoid errors that, more often than not, can be fairly costly. The following are some of the most common mistakes exhibitors make pre-show, at-show and post-show:

1. Failing to set exhibiting goals.
Goals, or the purpose for exhibiting, are the essence of the whole tradeshow experience. Knowing what you want to accomplish at a show will help plan every other aspect— your theme, the booth layout and display, graphics, product displays, premiums, literature, etc. Exhibiting goals should complement your corporate marketing objectives and help in accomplishing them.

2. Forgetting to read the exhibitor manual.
The exhibitor manual is your complete reference guide to every aspect of the show and your key to saving money. Admittedly, some show management make these easier to read than others. Albeit, everything you need to know about the show you are participating in, should be contained in the manual—show schedules, contractor information, registration, service order forms, electrical service, floor plans and exhibit specifications, shipping and freight services, housing information, advertising and promotion Remember that the floor price for show services is normally 10–20% higher so signing up early will always give you a significant savings.

3. Leaving graphics to the last minute.
Rush, change and overtime charges will add significantly to your bottom line. Planning your graphics in plenty of time - 6-8 weeks before show time will be less stressful for everyone concerned and avoids many blunders that occur under time pressures.

4. Neglecting booth staff preparation.
Enormous time, energy and money are put into organizing show participation - display, graphics, literature, premiums, etc. However, the people chosen to represent the entire image of the organization are often left to fend for themselves. They are just told to show up. Your people are your ambassadors and should be briefed beforehand - why you are exhibiting; what you are exhibiting and what you expect from them. Exhibit staff training is essential for a unified and professional image.

5. Ignoring visitors' needs.
Often staff members feel compelled to give the visitor as much information as possible. They fail to ask about real needs and interest in the product/service. They lack questioning skills and often miss important qualifying information. Pre-show preparation and training is the key.

6. Handing out literature and premiums.
Staff members, who are unsure of what to do in the booth environment or feel uncomfortable talking to strangers, end up handing out literature or giveaway items just to keep occupied. Literature acts as a barrier to conversation and chances are, will be discarded at the first opportunity. It is vital that people chosen to represent the organization enjoy interacting with strangers and know what is expected of them in the booth environment.

7. Being unfamiliar with demonstrations.
Many times staffers show up for duty only to discover they are totally unfamiliar with booth demonstrations.

Communicate with your team members before the show and ensure that demonstrators know what is being presented, are familiar with the equipment and how to conduct the assigned demonstrations.

8. Overcrowding the booth with company representatives.
Companies often send several representatives to major industry shows to gather competitive and general/specific industry information. These people feel compelled to gather at the company booth not only outnumbering visitors, but also monopolizing staffer time and restricting visitor interaction. Have strict rules regarding employees visiting the show and insist staffers not scheduled for booth duty stay away until their assigned time. Company executives are often the worst offenders. Assign specific tasks to avoid them fumbling around the booth.

9. Ignoring lead follow-up.
Show leads often take second place to other management activities that occur after being out of the office for several days. The longer leads are left unattended, the colder and more mediocre they become. Prior to the show, establish how leads will be handled, set timelines for follow-up and make sales representatives accountable for leads given to them.

10. Overlooking show evaluation.
The more you know and understand about your performance at shows, the more improvement and fine-tuning can take place for future shows. No two shows are alike. Each has it own idiosyncrasies and obstacles. There is always room for improvement. Invest the time with your staff immediately after each show to evaluate your performance. It pays enormous dividends.

Susan Friedmann, CSP (Certified Speaking Professional), The Tradeshow Coach, Lake Placid, NY, author, "Meeting & Event Planning for Dummies," works with exhibitors, show organizers and meeting planners to create more valuable results from their events nationally and internationally. Website: www.thetradeshowcoach.com

5 Reasons Manufacturers Should Offer Financing To Their Customers

One of the lingering negative effects of the recession on companies has been the decreased availability of access to capital. The following are five key reasons to consider offering financing to your customers.

1. It's a Growing Trend
A study by the Equipment Leasing & Finance Foundation shows that among manufacturers who offer financing for their equipment, approximately 30 percent of all equipment sales are financed by the manufacturer or its finance partner. That rate is increasing each year as the financing division plays a more important role in the organization's overall strategy. According to the same study, of all manufacturers who offer a financing option to their customers, 67 percent expect equipment financing will increase as a percentage of their manufacturer sales. The growth of this trend is largely due to the benefits derived from offering financing and its business impact.

2. It Builds Customer Relationships
Building customer relationships and improving customer retention are key benefits of establishing a finance capability. It allows you to build rapport and trust in addressing customers' financial issues, as well as answering their questions about the equipment. It also extends the relationship into future transactions since it provides opportunities to offer advice and assistance with end-of-lease/financing term decisions such as whether to purchase new or existing equipment. In addition to developing

follow-up selling opportunities, it helps build long-term relationships for repeat business.

3. It Provides Incremental Income

Providing a financing option can provide benefits including facilitating equipment sales and generating additional revenue. In addition to an increase in interest income, additional revenue may be generated if the equipment can be sold for more than its remaining book value at the end of lease.

4. It Creates Value

Offering financing creates value for your customers by saving them money, getting them better terms and helping them stay current. One way they save money is through the manufacturer's knowledge of the equipment and ability to resell pre-owned equipment. This may enable the manufacturer to take additional risks on the residual value which lowers the customer's monthly payment. Customers may get better terms when they purchase equipment that might be otherwise delayed because of lack of financing elsewhere, and the manufacturer is willing to provide better financing terms. Additionally, value is created when a customer takes advantage of leasing/financing since it eliminates the risk of them owning equipment that is technologically obsolete.

5. Industry Expertise is Available to Assist You

An important consideration about offering financing is that there is plenty of assistance that can help you determine and establish the captive financing option that's appropriate for your business. The Manufacturer & Vendor Resource Center (http://www.elfaonline.org/resources/MVRC/) contains strategic, legal, financial and operational topics manufacturers should consider when developing or enhancing their finance capability. The website also contains searchable databases to find financing partners and service providers to assist you. Increasing knowledge of captive financing among small and medium-sized manufacturers and vendors will prepare the way to greater growth opportunities for their businesses and the economy.

William G. Sutton, CAE, is President and CEO of the Equipment Leasing and Finance Association (elfaonline.org), the trade association that represents companies in the $725 billion equipment finance sector, which includes financial services companies and manufacturers engaged in financing capital goods. ELFA has been equipping business for success for more than 50 years.

20 Top Tips For Doing Business In China

Tip #1: Guanxi, or personal relationships, are of vital importance when doing business in China. Do not underestimate the importance of the relationship building process.

Tip #2: People are comfortable building relationships with honourable people who show respect to those to whom respect is due.

Tip #3: As all relationships are unequal it is important, if you wish to appear honourable, to show respect to age, seniority and educational background.

Tip #4: Managers tend to be directive, which reflects basic Confucian concepts of the hierarchical nature of society.

Tip #5: In return for loyalty, the boss is expected to show consideration and interest in all aspects of a subordinates' life.

Tip #6: There are often close relationships between senior management of a company and local party officials.

Tip #7: It is important that you do not make people 'lose face' in front of their group. Always respect seniority and do not openly disagree with people.

Tip #8: Do as many favors for people as possible - debts must always be repaid.

Tip #9: Business cards should be formally exchanged at the beginning of meetings. Treat the business card with great respect, as the card is the man.

Tip #10: Meetings are often long and seemingly without clear objectives. Very often the meeting is an exercise in relationship-building and the aim of the meeting is to move the relationship, rather than any specific business task, forward.

Tip #11: It can take several, very long meetings before any tangible progress is made. Patience is essential if you wish to capitalise on the situation.

Tip #12: The Chinese are very interested in long-term commitment. Build long-term goals and objectives into your proposals.

Tip #13: Do not be too direct. Strive for diplomacy, consensus and harmony. Remember that this takes time to achieve.

Tip #14: Do not assume comprehension. It is often useful to go over the same point several times from different angles in order to aid comprehension.

Tip #15: It is difficult for the Chinese to say 'no' directly. Anything other than a direct 'yes' could mean 'no'. Be circumspect and reflect on seeming agreements reached. Has an agreement actually been reached?

Tip #16: It is difficult to read body language as, by western standards, it is somewhat muted in China. Be very alive to any changes of posture, animation etc.

Tip #17: Gift giving is an everyday part of Chinese business culture. Giving and receiving gifts helps to cement relationships. Take gifts with you when visiting and put some thought and effort into the gift selection process.

Tip #18: Always wrap gifts before giving them. Gifts are rarely opened in front of the giver.

Tip #19: The Chinese are an intensely patriotic race. Do not make disparaging remarks about China, the political situation, human rights etc.

Tip #20: Entertaining is very important in the relationship building process. If entertaining, do it well. If being entertained at a banquet, take your lead from your hosts - they will enjoy taking you through the process.

Keith Warburton is the owner and founder of Global Business Culture, a cultural awareness training and consultancy firm based out of the U.K. Keith is a world-renowned expert on multiculturalism and a strategic partner of Bridge Consulting International. He can be reached at www.globalbusinessculture.com.

Chapter 5: Your Financials

9 Ways To Keep Your Business Overhead Under Control

Every business owner knows that it's critical to keep track of expenses. Keeping costs under wraps could mean the difference between staying in business or filing for bankruptcy. Our expert, a small business consultant and author, provides this list of ways to keep these costs from spiraling out of control.

1. Read your general ledger
It ain't a good beach read....but your general ledger will sure tell you a lot about your business. Every month you should print out a full detailed general ledger of all of your company's transactions and read through it. You'll be surprised what tidbits you'll find.

2. Get a Flash Report
Each day have your accounting manager give you a 'flash' report of open receivables, payables, sales, purchases and other critical metrics. Compare them to the prior day and week. Anything unusual will be sure to crop up and you can address before it becomes a bigger problem.

3. Start walking around
Get off your butt and walk around the office. Listen to what your employees are talking about. By walking around you'll see the action from a front row seat. You'll get back to you seat with a few more cost control ideas.

4. Start paying early and on specific days
Take advantage of vendor discounts. Set a specific payment schedule and stick to it. This way you can manage your cash flow on your timeline, not someone else's.

5. Outsource
There are so many ways a small business can keep costs under control just by outsourcing. Hire a payroll service. Farm out some manufacturing process. Subcontract a specific job.

6. Monitor revenue by employee
Productivity is the key to cost control. Each employee should be contributing to the overall revenue engine of your company. Don't add employees unless their contribution fuels your growth. Keep track of this number monthly and you'll keep up with your costs too.

7. Join a group
No matter what business you're in there's a group to join. Look for chambers of commerce, associations, fraternal organizations...whatever. Many of these groups offer volume discounts on health insurance and other typical business costs to their members. Joining a group is a great way to keep things under control.

8. Avoid and remove the corporate trappings
Do you really need that fancy office space? That state of the art computer system? Some companies, like corporate law or accounting firms, may need to impress. But won't your customers be happier with just good service and quality products? Don't overspend on corporate mish-mush that doesn't add to your bottom line.

9. Decide between 'nice to have' and 'must have'
Do you really need gourmet coffee in the office? Expensive copy paper? Multiple digital cameras? A super powerful computer? Don't buy into the hype of your supplier. Figure out what you really need to have and avoid the nice to have stuff, unless you can really justify that it's worth spending the money.

Gene Marks *(www.genemarks.com) is a small business owner and writes weekly for the New York Times, Forbes, and Inc.*

10 More Ways For Decreasing Your Overhead

Every business, no matter how large or how small, looks for ways to decrease expenses. Some are in financial crisis and need to do it to survive. Others would just like to have higher profit. Here are a few popular ways to accomplish the task.

1. Employee layoffs. - I have listed this first, because payroll is typically the largest single expense next to cost of goods sold, and it is the first place that employers look to cut. However, this can be a drastic step, and it can influence things such as employee morale, reputation, and unemployment costs. Before you take this course, make sure you have examined all of your other options.

2. Change health benefits. - With health insurance soaring twenty percent per year, this is an area that gets expensive fast. Always make sure that the employee contributes something, even if it is a token amount. If not, there will be no incentive for the employee to be covered under the spouse's insurance, and you will end up footing the bill. Increasing deductibles and co-pays are small but effective ways to decrease health care costs.

3. Purchase in quantity. - If you are in a manufacturing or distribution business, your suppliers normally have volume discounts. Even if you have no room to store the excess product, it is sometimes cheaper to rent a small warehouse, depending on the size of the discount. Also, try purchasing from a cooperative or a large consumer warehouse store.

4. Reduce credit card fees. - If you sell to the public, it is almost imperative to accept credit and debit cards. The fees accompanying them can be overwhelming, but the good news is that there is tremendous competition in the credit card processing field. Have different companies give you quotes, but make sure you know ALL of their charges. Most importantly, ask them if there is a charge to cancel their contract.

5. Cut travel expenses. - In the old days, the only way to have a meeting with someone out of town was to travel. Now, technology has provided other means, such as teleconferencing, video conferencing, internet interfacing, etc. These can be just as effective at a fraction of the cost. They also cut employee downtime and add productivity to existing staff, allowing you to decrease personnel.

6. Eliminate company cars. - Change from a company car to a car allowance. This puts the onus of controlling auto expenses on the employee. It is a disincentive to using the company car for personal reasons, or to schedule unnecessary business trips. Unsafe drivers do not cause an increase in company insurance costs. If the employee exceeds his/her car allowance, the expenses are still potentially deductible, but the travel expenses for the business are capped.

7. Cut advertising costs. - Do you really need that big Yellow Pages ad? Reevaluating advertising efficiency could direct your budgeted dollars in a different direction, resulting in either increased revenues or reduced costs. Don't place ads just because everyone else does. Make sure they are working for you.

8. Evaluate telephone costs. - With the advent of cell phones, pagers and personal data assistants, communication costs have skyrocketed. Many companies offer group plans or service combinations that take advantage of economies of scale. In addition, it is important to reexamine your main switchboard setup to see if it is as efficient as possible.

9. Refinance loans. - Startup companies typically do not have the bargaining power to get the best loan terms from lending institutions. As your business matures, you should revisit your existing loans to see if refinancing can lower debt service costs. It may even be possible for the business owner to take out an inexpensive home equity loan and lend the money to the company.

10. Relocate to smaller offices. - As companies grow technologically, their space needs may actually decrease. Converting some employees to telecommuters can also decrease the amount of office space necessary. If your lease term is nearing an end, it may make sense to move to smaller quarters.

David A. Caplan, CPA, MBA has clients geographically located all over the United States. His website is www.caplancpa.com. He can be reached at P.O. Box 301, Lafayette Hill, PA 19444, Tel: (610) 834-5754, Fax: (610) 834-1013.

6 Calculations For Measuring A Manufacturer's Financial Health

No matter what type of business you're in, or what your educational background is, if you want to succeed you've got to have a working knowledge of these basic financial concepts

1. The basic set of financial statements - The basic set of financial statements are the Balance Sheet, Income Statement (also known as the Profit & Loss Statement) and Statement of Cash Flows. Since business results are measured in dollars, it's imperative that you know how to read the basic set of financial statements. Sadly, many smaller business owners wait to learn about financial statements whenever they need to borrow money. Instead, they tend to focus on components or specific accounts such as cash, accounts receivable, inventory, office expense, payroll, and so forth. While this may be fine when first starting out, it isn't nearly enough if you want to grow your business. In order to grow, it's essential to see the whole picture. Being able to understand your company's basic financial statements is the first step in mastering your company's finances.

2. Cash flow projections – Cash flow projections have the same purpose as the statement of cash flows: to keep track of cash. The only difference is that cash flow projections help you deal with the future while the statement of cash flow shows how you've managed cash in the past. The ability to manage your company's cash is vital to its success. A cash flow projection is an important financial tool that will help you accomplish that goal. It surprises me how many smaller business owners don't adequately measure and project cash flow. For many, a casual glance at their checkbook balance is the extent of their cash flow management. Unfortunately, looking at and balancing your checkbook is not the same thing as measuring or projecting cash flow. If you run your business solely by looking at your checking account balance, you're making a critical mistake. A checking account balance represents the past and present. In order to successfully manage cash flow you need to deal with the future. You need to know how much money you're going to collect and how much you're going to spend. That's the essence of projecting cash flow. In addition, a cash flow projection shows you where the money is "tied up" in your business.

3. Ratio analysis - If you're not financial ratio savvy, you're not alone! Many smaller business owners aren't. **But then again many smaller business owners aren't as successful as they should be!** The fact is, knowledge of even just a few key ratios goes a long way in increasing your ability to analyze and understand your company's financial position. Ratios allow you to see things that would otherwise be hidden from the naked eye. The information suggested by financial ratios can help you to improve results, especially profitability. By analyzing changes and trends over time, ratios allow you to pinpoint and improve specific problem areas. They do a much better job of isolating these areas than do the basic set of financial statements alone. In addition, a ratio becomes an even more powerful tool if you compare it to the ratios of other companies in the same industry (see the next item, Trend Analysis).

4. Trend analysis - Now let's take ratio analysis one-step further. Even though ratios are excellent financial management tools, they're limited because they ignore the time dimension. Success (or failure) tends to be something that happens over a period of time, not in one or two moments. Since ratios are snapshots at one point in time, they may not, by themselves, be able to detect trends or patterns. As I just mentioned, ratios are even more powerful when compared and analyzed over time in order to derive meaningful results. That's where trend analysis comes into play. Trend analysis happens to be one of my all time favorite management tools. It's cost effective and easy to learn. It can help you to spot either emerging opportunities or impending difficulties. There's no doubt that you need to stay on top of trends in order to build a gold mine business. Trend analysis is simply taking a look at financial and other data, including ratios, and trying to recognize or interpret patterns. In addition, trends can be compared to industry averages, or used in the development of company budgets and forecasts.

5. Forecasts, projections & budgets - Forecasts, projections and budgets are reports designed to help you compare anticipated future events with actual results. They are indispensable financial management tools. A budget, for example, can tell you a whole host of things like how many employees you can afford or how much money can be spent on advertising and promotions. Unfortunately, so few smaller businesses actually utilize one on a regular basis. Forecasts and projections show how your business will turn out under various assumptions. This analysis is critical if you want to grow. For example, a projection can be used to measure a company's expected financial position once it gets required financing. A budget is very similar to a forecast or projection in that it also involves predicting the future. A budget will help you to understand why some of your plans didn't turn out as expected. This is because once a budget is prepared it can be compared to actual results to determine variances. These variances can be investigated and scrutinized. A budget can also be used to help you control costs and manage resources.

6. Break-even analysis - Break-even analysis is where you determine the point of activity (sales volume) where total revenues and total expenses are equal. In other words, the break-even point shows you the minimum amount of sales you need to cover your expenses. Do you know your break-even levels? This tool is a MUST when launching a new product or service or when adjusting prices.

Alex Goumakos CPA (www.goldminetactics.com) business consultant and author of "Business Owner's Success Manual." His services help clients increase profits in their existing business or start a successful business from scratch. Contact him at MindStudio, Inc. 2402 Lisa Lane - Suite 200 Allentown PA 18104 USA, Phone: (888) 839-2727, Email: alex@goldminetactics.com

4 Purchasing Practices That Can Change A Manufacturer's Life

If a low price is guiding most of your purchasing decisions, you'll find that your role is more like a babysitter than a purchasing professional.

1. Work with fewer suppliers - I know this seems counter-intuitive. Many think that because it is easy to go out to bid to many suppliers (think BCC email) that that is how you get your best deal. The truth is that while you might find a one-time low price, you lose other valuable long-term benefits. If each one of your many suppliers is only receiving a small fraction of your work, you will not be able to realize savings based on scale nor will you receive the level of service that you could be enjoying from suppliers who are working hard to reward your loyalty. Cultivate a few good suppliers and build a feeling of partnership with them and you'll find that your costs will be in control and your job will be a lot easier.

2. Provide good information - Nothing is harder to hit than a target that is moving or barely visible. If you don't know clearly what you want, how can your suppliers ever satisfy you. In today's manufacturing environment, data - good data - is essential. Gone are the days where projects are built from a sketch on a napkin. For our production metal fabrication company, having accurate digital part data is a must. From calculating accurate laser cutting times and sheet yields for estimating, to programming our multi-axis lasers and press brakes, we operate best when we have the right type of information. You'll find that the extra effort you put in making sure your suppliers have data that is clear, complete, accurate and in the right format will not only make them happy, but their improved efficiency will mean greater savings and fewer headaches for you.

3. Share the big picture - Most of the time suppliers are kept on a need-to-know basis (and they don't need to know). It's as if what's happening in your company is top secret information and they don't have the right security clearance. In this environment, when they are bidding on a specific project, they are only looking at a small part of the overall plan. But often times, if a supplier understands your overall objectives and can see what you are looking to accomplish over the next weeks, months or even years, they are able to craft solutions that can help you accomplish your goals rather than just submitting proposals that focus only on the immediate need. You'll find that good, informed suppliers can actually be powerful allies.

4. Make quality your highest priority - Price, Delivery and Quality. That's what everyone wants, right? For sure, each one of these is very important, but I have found that the one you consider most important will drive a particular type of results.If delivery is your key priority, then, while you might be getting your products in quickly, you may be paying premium for this benefit and quality may be sacrificed for speed. If a low price is guiding most of your purchasing decisions, you'll find that your role is more like a babysitter than a purchasing professional. Your up-front savings will be lost when the parts have to get reworked or when production is delayed waiting on those "cheap" parts to arrive.

Gary Weldon has spent his entire 25 year career in the manufacturing industry. His roles, however, have been widely varied. Through a combination of hard work, hands-on experience and education he was able to move from shop go-fer to shop foreman in just ten years. From there he ventured into tooling and machinery design, purchasing and, ultimately, operations management. He is also the co-founder and editor of MADEinDAYTONblog.com, a popular blog that champions manufacturing in the Dayton, Ohio region.

11 Most Common Insurance Coverages For The Manufacturer

Most manufacturers know they need insurance to protect their business from a variety of risks. This list summarizes the primary insurance coverages to consider. It is important to work with a qualified insurance agent, who can help you identify the appropriate coverage based on the specific needs of your business.

1. General Liability – In today's litigious society, virtually any business that invites the public onto its premises, provides a service or manufactures a product is vulnerable to a lawsuit claiming injury or damage. Liability insurance provides coverage for a business's assets, if the company is sued for something it did or failed to do that resulted in bodily injury or property damage to someone else. Specific types of coverage include:

- **Bodily Injury** – For injuries or deaths that occur on a company's property or arise from its operations.
- **Property Damage** – For damage to someone else's property.
- **Product and Completed Operations** – For bodily injury or property damage to others caused by a company's finished work or manufactured goods.
- **Personal and Advertising Injury** – For lawsuits brought against the company alleging libel, slander, false arrest, malicious prosecution, wrongful eviction, discrimination, or violation of the right of privacy. May also include coverage for claims of copyright infringement in company advertising.

2. Property – Property insurance is a critical coverage for manufacturers. It not only provides coverage for costs associated with repairing or replacing buildings and other property owned or used by the business, but it can also provide protection from indirect losses, such as lost profits or extra expenses, that arise after direct damage to property from a covered cause of loss. Specific coverage options include:

- **Buildings and Business Personal Property** – For buildings and personal property used by the business, whether the manufacturer owns or is responsible for it.

- **Equipment Breakdown** – For the cost to repair or replace critical equipment that breaks down or is damaged due to specified mechanical or electrical causes.

- **Ordinance or Law** – For loss to the undamaged portion of a building, demolition costs and increased costs of construction when required by building codes, ordinances or laws.

- **Business Income** – For lost income due to the interruption of business operations from a covered cause of loss. Extra Expense coverage pays for additional expenses incurred that exceed normal expenses following a covered loss. Civil Authority coverage replaces lost income when access to an insured's business is prohibited by an order of Civil Authority due to a covered cause of loss.

- **Utility Service Interruption**— For lost income and extra expenses resulting from a covered disruption of utility service.

- **Computers and Media** — For a manufacturer's computer equipment, media and data. Options may include coverage for replacement of damaged equipment and payment for lost income due to the interruption of business operations by a covered cause of loss.

- **Manufacturers Selling Price**–In the event of a covered loss to finished goods, provides payment based on the selling price of the damaged item.

3. Marine – Property and liability coverage for a variety of specialized needs, such as Ocean Cargo or Shipper's Interest.

4. Workers' Compensation – Provides coverage for medical costs and lost wages associated with an employee's work-related injury. It is important to choose a workers' compensation insurer that offers appropriate loss control and claims management services to assist employers in preventing workplace injuries and illnesses and help injured employees return to work as quickly as medically appropriate.

5. Commercial Auto – Property and liability coverage for vehicles owned by a company for business purposes. Two important coverage options include Hired Auto liability, which provides coverage for bodily injury or property damage arising out of the use or maintenance of a hired auto by an insured or its employees; and Non-Owned Auto liability coverage, which typically provides coverage for bodily injury and property damage on an excess basis for liability resulting from the use of "non-owned autos," such as employees driving their personal vehicles for company business.

6. Umbrella – Liability coverage in excess of a company's primary liability policies (General Liability, Commercial Auto) in the event of a catastrophic claim. Coverage is typically tailored to the underlying policies.

7. International - For manufacturers conducting business outside of the U.S., it is important to consider international coverage for various risks, as exposures may be different in foreign jurisdictions. These can include general liability and products liability; auto liability, including rental exposures; business personal property, including property in transit; international travel and medical assistance; accidental death and dismemberment; kidnap and extortion; and employer's responsibility, which provides protection for employees who are injured or contract a disease while traveling or conducting business overseas.

8. Manufacturers' Errors & Omissions – Liability coverage for claims alleging economic loss suffered as a result of a manufacturing mistake. These losses are typically not covered by a general liability policy.

9. Product Recall Expense – For costs associated with a product recall, such as product repair or replacement costs; mail and media announcements, additional staff, storage, and disposal expenses, if special disposal is required, as well as expenses incurred by third party acting on the manufacturer's behalf and good faith advertising to regain customer trust.

10. Data Breach – Virtually any business that collects or stores sensitive customer or employee information can be vulnerable to a data breach. Data breach policies typically offer first-party coverage for expenses incurred in responding to and managing a data breach, such as notification expenses, crisis management and credit monitoring services. Options for third-party defense and liability coverage may provide defense and indemnification when an insured is legally responsible for a data breach. Some policies also offer access to consultative and legal services to help a business assess, prevent and respond to a breach.

11. Employee Benefits - While healthcare reform has put focus on medical insurance, other insurance benefits can help a manufacturer recruit and retain employees. Life and disability insurance can help protect employees' family finances. Disability insurance also includes resources to help employees get back to an active, productive life following a disabling illness or off-the-job injury, such as a broken leg or sprained back. Another benefit to consider is accidental death & dismemberment insurance.

The Hartford is a leader in property and casualty insurance, group benefits and mutual funds. The company is widely recognized for its excellence, sustainability practices, trust and integrity. To learn more about The Hartford's insurance products and services for manufacturers, visit www.thehartford.com

14 Things A Manufacturer Should Remember When Filing for A Patent

Filing a patent is a time consuming and complex process. Not doing things the right way can set your timetable back many months. Our experts know everything about this process—they invented it! Here some important considerations when filing for your patent.

1. When filing under unavoidable or unintentional standards
Petitions to revive filed under either the unavoidable or the unintentional standards should be filed within **two months** of becoming aware of the abandonment of the application to avoid any question of timeliness.

2. Renewed petitions
Renewed petitions to revive must be filed **within two months** of an **adverse decision** on the earlier petition to revive to be considered timely, unless a proper extension of time up to an additional five months (for a total of seven months) is obtained under 37 CFR 1.136(a). Otherwise, the Office may require a specific showing as to how the entire delay was unavoidable or unintentional.

3. Petition fees
A petition under 37 CFR 1.137(a) must be accompanied by the **petition fee** set forth in 37 CFR 1.17(l) and a petition under 37 CFR 1.137 (b) must be accompanied by the petition fee set forth in 37 CFR 1.17(m). The petition fee is required by **statute**. See 35 U.S.C. 41(a)(7). Thus, the Office cannot grant requests for waiver or reduction of the requisite petition fee.

4. Non-provisional applications
In a **non-provisional** application abandoned for failure to prosecute, the required reply may be met by the filing of a **continuing application** .

5. Issue fees
In an application abandoned for failure to pay the issue fee or any portion thereof, the required reply must be the payment of the **issue fee** or any **outstanding balance** thereof even if the application is to then be abandoned in favor of a continuing application. In a patent lapsed for failure to pay the balance of issue fee due, the required reply is payment of the balance of issue fee due.

6. Office requirement
In a **provisional** application abandoned for failure to timely comply with an Office requirement, the reply requirement must be met by a **complete reply** to such Office requirement.

7. Abandoned applications
37 CFR 1.137(b) is applicable to applications abandoned and patents lapsed, regardless of the length of time that the application was abandoned or the patent was lapsed. However, note that 37 CFR 1.137(b) requires that the **entire period of delay**, from the due date of the reply to the date of filing a grantable petition to revive, was **unintentional** for a petition under 37 CFR 1.137(b) to be granted.

8. Statement of unintentional delay
While a statement of **unintentional** delay for the entire period of abandonment is generally sufficient, 37 CFR 1.137(b) authorizes the Office to require additional information when there is a question whether the entire delay was unintentional. In such instances, the Office may require evidence for each of the three critical periods: (1) the delay in filing a **timely** *reply* before abandonment of the application or lapse of the patent; (2) the delay in filing an

initial petition to revive; and (3) the delay in filing a **grantable petition** to revive.

9. Deliberately delaying the filing

An applicant who deliberately delays the filing of a petition under 37 CFR 1.137 will not be able to show that "the entire delay in filing the required reply from the due date of the reply until the filing of a grantable petition pursuant to 37 CFR 1.137(b) was unintentional".

10. Examples of situations with unintentional delay

Examples of situations where unintentional delay was argued but the Office held these activities to constitute **intentional delay**: (A) where the applicant **deliberately permits** an application to become **abandoned** (i.e., due to a conclusion that the claims are unpatentable, that a rejection in an Office action cannot be overcome, or that an invention lacks sufficient commercial value to justify continued prosecution); (B) where the applicant **chooses not to seek or persist in seeking revival** of an abandoned application, or where the applicant deliberately chooses to delay seeking revival of an abandoned application;

11. Intentional delay

An **intentional delay** resulting from a deliberate course of action chosen by the applicant *is* **not affected by:** (a) the correctness of the applicant (or applicant's representative) decision to abandon the application or not to seek or persist in seeking revival of the application; (b) the correctness or propriety of a rejection, or other objection, requirement, or decision by the Office; or (c) the discovery of new information or evidence, or other change in circumstances subsequent to the abandonment or decision not to seek or persist in seeking revival.

12. Intentional abandonment

An **intentional abandonment** of an application, or an **intentional delay** in seeking either the withdrawal of a holding of abandonment in, or the revival of, an abandoned application, precludes a finding of unavoidable or unintentional delay pursuant to 37 CFR 1.137.

13. When you choose not seek revival

Where an applicant **chooses not to** seek **revival** of an application, or chooses **not to persist in seeking revi**val after an adverse decision on an earlier petition, the resulting delay cannot be considered to be unavoidable or unintentional.

14. Provisional application

A **provisional** application can be revived for a period **not to exceed 12 months** from the **date of filing**, even if the petition is filed outside this 12 month period.

United States Patent And Trademark Office (www.uspto.gov)

6 Places To Conduct A Trademark Search

1. Trademark Acceptable Identification of Goods and Services Manual (Available in paper, DVD-ROM or on the USPTO Web)
Begin with this alphabetical listing of acceptable terms for the identification of goods and services. Locate terms that describe your good or service. For example, "flying discs" is the acceptable term for a flying saucer-type toy. Note the international class number listed next to each term. Also identify terms for goods and/or services that are used, advertised or sold with your product. For instance, peanut butter is sold and used with jellies and jams. Finally, check for deleted terms that may be related to your good or service.

2. International Schedule of Classes (Available in paper, DVD-ROM or on the Web)
Scan the schedule for additional classes that are related to your product or service. For instance, if your product is income tax preparation software, Class 36 would be related because it includes services related to insurance, financial affairs, monetary affairs and real estate. The schedule is located on the back cover of the *Basic Facts About Trademarks* booklet.

3. Trademark Manual of Examining Procedure (TMEP) (Available in paper, DVD-ROM or on the USPTO Web)
Review Chapter 1400 for the appropriate class scope notes in order to confirm the terms and classes you have chosen. For example, Class 8 (Hand Tools) includes cutlery but not surgical knives, which are in Class 10 (Medical Apparatus),

or fencing weapons, which are found in Class 28 (Toys and Sporting Goods).

4. Design Code Manual (Available in paper or on the USPTO Web)
If your mark incorporates a design or logo you must search for trademarks that might be confusingly similar. Use the index in the back of the *Design Code Manual* to locate the appropriate six-digit code for each design element in your mark. For example, a logo depicting an eagle would be coded 03.15.01. Each element in a logo is assigned a design code. Carefully review the guidelines for each category.

5. Trademarks REGISTERED and PENDING DVD-ROMs or the Trademark Electronic Search System (TESS) (Available on DVD-ROM or on the USPTO Web)
Conduct the search combining your word mark or logo with the terms, classes and design codes you've identified in steps 1-4. Remember to search for alternate spellings, phonetic and foreign language equivalents, synonyms and homonyms. For example, SNOW BRITE, SNOW BRIGHT, SNO-BRITE, SNO-BRIGHT, SNOW WHITE, etc.

6. TARR Trademark Status Database (Available on the USPTO Web only)
Finally, check TARR, the *Trademark Applications & Registrations Retrieval* system, for the current status of the marks you found in Step 5. Records in the Web trademark databases are linked directly to their TARR equivalents. The TARR database is updated daily at 5 a.m. and contains important trademark application and registration information not found on CD-ROM, the Web or in the **Official Gazette** .

The United States Patent and Trademark Office, uspto.gov

10 Federal Tax Benefits Specifically For Manufacturers

This list summarizes some of the tax benefit strategies available to manufacturing businesses.

1. **Credit for Increasing Research Activities (R&D Credit) – Sec 41**
The credit is an incremental credit derived from the taxpayer's qualified research expenses (QREs) for the taxable year. QREs may include qualified wages, supplies, and contract research expenses.

2. **Interest Charge Domestic International Sales Corporation (IC-DISC) - Sec 991-997**
Taxpayers can convert a portion of their foreign sales income from ordinary income rates to the capital gains rate and thereby save on this arbitrage.

3. **Cost Segregation**
Taxpayers can segregate the different costs on their buildings and facilities to accelerate the depreciation and thereby get greater tax savings currently rather than depreciating over 30+ years.

4. **Research and Experimental Expenditures Deduction – Sec 174**
Taxpayers can treat non-capitalized research or experimental expenditures in connection with trade or business as expenses and are allowed as deductions.

5. Deduction for Qualified Domestic Production Activities Income – Sec 199

Taxpayers may deduct a percentage of their qualified production activities income (QPAI). QPAI is derived from the excess of the domestic production gross receipts over the sum of the cost of goods sold allocated to such receipts and other expenses, losses, or deductions allocated to such receipts.

6. Accelerated Depreciation for Qualified Capital Assets – Sec 168

Taxpayers may be generally allowed to recover the cost of qualified capital assets sooner than they can be recovered conventionally. Accelerated depreciation can be used when an asset is expected to be much more productive during its early years, so that depreciation expense is a more accurate representation of the asset's value.

7. Acceleration of the AMT and research credits in lieu of bonus depreciation – Sec 168(k)(4)

Manufacturers affected by the AMT may be able to take a refundable tax credit. Faced with losses and unused AMT credits, taxpayers may claim the optional refundable credit instead of bonus depreciation allowances that would only boost their losses.

8. Election to Expense Certain Depreciable Business Assets – Sec 179

Taxpayers can treat the cost of certain non-capitalized property as an expense, and allowed as a deduction for the taxable year placed in service.

9. Inventory Accounting by Last-In, First-Out (LIFO) Method – Sec 474

Highly beneficial to manufacturing firms facing inflating costs for inventory, this method allows them to reduce tax burdens on the difference between the sales price and the rising cost of inventories (thereby reflecting the correct profit).

10. Inventory Property Sales Source Rule Exception – Sec 865(b)

Domestic exporters are allowed an exception to the rule that income is sourced according to the seller's residence. U.S .manufacturing companies faced with foreign tax credits may use this exception to increase the amount of credits applied against their U.S. income tax liability.

Saqib Dhanani spearheads the audit defense division at Paradigm Partners (paradigmlp.com), where he manages a team of Tax Controversy Attorneys.

14 Key Issues When Buying A Manufacturing Business

1. What assurances are in place that the company can continue to manufacture domestically?
With the ongoing trends of manufacturing moving offshore from domestic facilities, can the company you will want to know what other like companies in the industry are doing and whether the business can remain competitive with continued domestic manufacturing

2. Does the company compete on price, quality, or service or have a process/product that is exclusive to them?
This is extremely important especially if the company competes on prices as that can be a volatile business model. Analyzing several years of financials will give you insight to the ability of the company to sustain revenue and profit levels.

3. Are there any customer concentration issues (this is a common problem)?
Do any of the customers represent a disproportionate percentage of the company's revenues/profits? Here again, you want to avoid volatile businesses than can decline dramatically with the exit of a few clients.

4. Do you have access to additional funds for future capital expenditures? On this note be sure to adjust the Owner's Benefit downwards to accommodate future capital expenditures.
Manufacturing businesses by nature are capital intensive. If machinery needs to be replaced can the present cash flow accommodate this expenditure? The adjustment for future

capital expenditures may need to be made against the depreciation that may be added back by the seller when presenting their financials upon which they have valued the business.

5. Is there pending technology that could render the product or process obsolete?
Technology can have a positive effect on a business but so too can the impact be a negative one. Are there any industry advances that could impact the way the company does or should operate, either positively or negatively?

6. Can the client base be expanded? How?
This of course is a critical element to determine potential growth opportunities. What can a new owner do to built expand the customer base?

7. Can you add new products to your offering?
Ideally, you will want to add new products to sell to the existing client base. It is an effective method to grow a business.

8. What is the condition of the equipment? Does it use the latest technology or is it antiquated?
This aspect is crucial. As mentioned earlier, manufacturing entails capital resources and the bottom line a buyer anticipates could change drastically if major investments need to be made to replace old or inefficient equipment.

9. How long can it be utilized and maintain current production levels?
This aspect examines the useful life of existing equipment to determine how long the company can operate at present production levels with the current equipment.

10. What does the owner do each day?
As a prospective new owner, you will want to get a solid grasp on what the current owner does each day in the business. What are their primary areas of responsibility and

can you effectively assume their role. Do you have the knowledge or experience to do so or will you need to hire a manager? If the latter, is that a feasible plan?

11. Are the systems up to date to manage the manufacturing process?
Business operational systems work in tandem with manufacturing equipment. The systems determine the processes, measurement and analysis. One without the other is simply operating blindly. Does the company have effective systems in place? If not, can new ones be implemented and at what cost?

12. You will want to learn about the typical "Work in Progress" levels since this almost always becomes an issue when closing the deal.
Often, negotiating the deal gets derailed when W-I-P is addressed. First, you need to know the financial amount involved at any one time. The seller will likely want to get paid for this component and ideally, you can do so at their cost or creatively structure the terms so the seller gets a percentage of the profit this W-I-P represents at the time of closing.

13. What sources does the company use for raw materials? Will they continue to sell to you and on what trade terms?
As part of the due diligence, you will need confirmation form suppliers of the trade terms under which they will continue to supply you with materials. If trade terms will change, you will need to potentially adjust cash flow and working capital projections and requirements.

14. Many industrialists have made fortunes in manufacturing. Despite the fact that we are shifting to a serviced based economy, there will always be certain industries where products require domestic manufacturing. Naturally, you will want to be certain

this is the case for any manufacturing business you consider purchasing. Ultimately, this is the big question today when considering the purchase of a manufacturing business. While growth is a wonderful objective, sustainability of the revenues and profits is the goal in the near term. The investigation of a business must go beyond the financials given the nature of current trends to be certain you are going to buy a business with a bright future and not one that will soon become one of the victims of offshore manufacturing.

Richard Parker – author of the How To Buy A Good Business At A Great Price© series. To read more articles by Richard visit Diomo.com or richardparker.com

7 Financial Terms Every Manufacturer Should Know

To help get you on the right financial footing to ensure confidence from your team and your investors, here are seven basic finance terms that every good manufacturer knows. We've also included a few additional resources to brush up on your Finance 101.

1. Bottom Line:
Net earnings and net income both fall under the "bottom line" description. You may hear people talk about "affecting the bottom line" of the company and this is simply any action that may increase or decrease the company's net earnings, or overall profit. The term "bottom" is in reference to the typical location of the number on a company's income statement, below both revenues (top line) and expenses. Needless to say, this is an important term to know.

2. Gross Margin:
Gross margin is expressed as a percentage and represents the percent of total sales revenue that a company keeps after subtracting the cost of producing its goods or services. The higher the percentage, the more the company keeps on each dollar of sales (that will eventually go toward paying its other costs and obligations). In simple terms, if a company's gross margins are 25 percent, for every dollar of revenue that is generated, the company will retain $0.25 before paying its overhead, which includes salaries, rent, and more.

3. Fixed versus Variable Costs:
A fixed cost is exactly what is sounds like, a cost that does not change with increases or decreases in the volume of goods or services that are produced by your company. These

costs are obviously the easiest to predict and plan for. Rent, salaries, and utilities all usually fall into this category.

Variable costs are just the opposite. They can vary depending on what a company is producing (such as Amazon Web Services usage), and as a result are much harder to forecast.

4. Equity versus Debt:
The "equity versus debt" comparison may seem silly to some, but you would be surprised at how many people I have come across who have no idea what either really means. Equity is simply money obtained from investors in exchange for ownership of a company, while debt comes in the form of loans from banks that must be repaid over time. Both are necessary for growth, with their own pros and cons. Equity versus debt is a critical decision for any entrepreneur and it is important to know the difference as the future of your business may depend on it.

5. Leverage:
Leverage can be interpreted a couple different ways. In the financial world, leverage is most commonly known as the amount of debt that can be used to finance your business' assets. In simple terms, the amount of money you borrowed to run your business. The balance you want to strike as an entrepreneur is that of your debt and equity. If you have way more debt than equity, you will be considered "highly leveraged" aka "very risky" to potential investors.

6. Capital Expenditures (CapEx):
Capital expenditures are any items purchased by your business that create future benefits. Basically, if something you bought is going to be useful to your business beyond the taxable year in which you purchased it, capitalize the item(s) as assets in your accounting. Examples include computers, property, or acquisitions.

7. Concentration:

Concentration is simply the measure (usually a percentage) of how much business you are doing with a specific client or partner. Relying on one or a couple of clients and partners to do business is a prime example of over-concentration. This is a losing strategy for any business because if something goes wrong with those limited relationships your business will be in serious trouble. Focus on keeping low concentrations for your accounts and investors will be impressed.

Jed Simon is the founder and CEO of FastPay (gofastpay.com), an online finance platform providing lines of credit to digital businesses.

4 Great Manufacturing Blogs To Follow

1. **From One Engineer to Another®** – International premier materials supplier Indium has more than a dozen of its engineers writing blogs under the banner "From One Engineer to Another." They proudly use the language of engineering to explain what Indium's products do. (www.indium.com/videos/from-one-engineer-to-another)

2. **The 21st Century Supply Chain** – Supply chain automation software company Kinaxis set out to double their leads and website visitors via an aggressive social media policy. They have increased web traffic by 2.7 times, and leads by 3.1 times. The 21st Century Supply Chain Blog features 18 contributors and focuses on thought leadership. (blog.kinaxis.com)

3. **Made In Dayton Blog** — Steve Staub, of Staub Manufacturing Solutions in Dayton, Ohio, created the Made In Dayton Blog to offer expert advice and tips for manufacturers in the Dayton area and elsewhere. The blog also covers news that affects local manufacturing. Not only does Staub's blog exhibit a sense of localized pride and help build community amongst Dayton manufacturers, it establishes Staub as a leading voice representing one of the United States' most significant manufacturing centers. (www.madeindaytonblog.com)

4. **Industrial Marketing Today** – Written by Anchinta Mitra for his Houston-based company Tiecas, Inc., Industrial Marketing Today shares Mitra's insights on aspects of the marketing world that are often unique to both industrial and manufacturing industries, emphasizing business-to-business relationships. (industrialmarketingtoday.com)

Once an aspiring cartoonist, **Will Silvey Simons** *settled into the world of the written word after earning a BA in English in 2006, shortly thereafter spending several years on staff at an alt-weekly in Omaha, working his way up to the managing editor position. He went on to co-found Omahype.com, an online publication calendar currently serving up culture to the greater Omaha area and beyond.*

7 Things To Include In Your Break Even Analysis

A significant advantage of some business ideas is that the venture can break even at what seems to be an easily achievable volume. A technique for quantifying that volume, called break-even analysis, examines the interaction among fixed costs, variable costs, prices, and unit volume to determine that combination of elements in which revenues and total costs are equal. Here are some items you should include in your break even analysis.

1. Fixed costs
Fixed costs are those expenses necessary to keep the business open, and are not impacted by sales volume. They will include such things as rent, basic telephone expenses and utilities, wages for core employees, loan or lease payments, and other necessary expenditures. An entrepreneur should also include a living wage for himself/herself as a fixed cost.

2. Salaries Expense
Did we figure in the company's obligation on payroll taxes? Did you allow for additional wages to cover vacations and sick days? Are you providing any benefits? Are you using a payroll service?

3. Occupancy Expense
In addition to rent, have you included likely utilities costs? Which are you liable for? Electricity, gas, garbage disposal, and telephone are usually the major ones. Don't forget long-distance calls. Is there Internet service?

4. Sales Expense

Have you determined your advertising costs? Are their printing costs? Cell phones probably should be charged here.

5. Other

Some of the more frequently overlooked costs include insurance, fees to professionals (legal, accounting, other), and interest payments.

6. Variable costs

Variable costs include those expenses that change as a result of sales volume. This can be a relatively simple relationship, as in cost of goods sold, where for example the variable cost of baked goods sold at our coffee shop is what we pay the supplier for them, $0.30 each. Variable costs can also be very complex; for example, higher sales in one area of our business may increase long distance charges. Labor costs may be fixed for full-time employees, then, as sales increase, some overtime is incurred until additional personnel can be justified.

7. Contribution margin

A general term often used for the difference between selling price and variable cost is "contribution margin," or the amount that the unit sale contributes to the margin available to pay fixed costs, and hopefully generate profit.

Dr. John B. Vinturella of Vinturella and Associates, (www.jbv.com), a management consulting firm specializing in entrepreneurs and small business. Dr. Vinturella, company principal, has almost 40 years experience as a management and strategic consultant and entrepreneur, and 15 of those years as an academic Entrepreneur-in-Residence and Adjunct Professor. He can be reached at (504) 246-3999, and at jbv@jbv.com. His address is 11111 Winchester Park Drive, New Orleans, LA 70128.

7 Ways to Get the Most Out Of Your Financial Statements

If you ask small business owners what's their least favorite part of running their businesses, most will probably say to you that it's managing the finances. But without sound financial management, any business, regardless of its size, won't be around for long. This starts with an understanding of basic financial statements and what they can tell you about the financial performance of your company. Here are a few tips for getting the most out of your firm's financial statements:

1. Determine whether or not you need to create financial statements

Any business that files a corporate tax return (partnerships and C and S corporations) must create a balance sheet and income statement. Along with a cash flow statement, these comprise the three types of business financial statements. If you apply for a bank loan or any other type of financing, you will need to present credible financial statements. If you're a sole proprietor and only file a Schedule C with your federal tax return, financial statements aren't required, but they can be an invaluable financial management tool.

2. Understand the differences between the three types of financial statements

The balance sheet is simply a snapshot of your financial position at any given point in time. Usually presented in two columns, it reflects what your company owns (assets) vs. what your company owes (liabilities). The income statement (or P&L) tells you how much money you made (or lost) for a given period of time—usually a month, quarter or year. And the cash flow statement ties the balance sheet and income statement together, reconciling the change in your business' cash position from the beginning to the end of the period being measured (usually a year). In short, it tells you where cash came from and what the business did with it.

3. Know what your balance sheet is telling you
The three most valuable pieces of information you can glean from the balance sheet are how liquid the company is, how much debt the company is using, and how quickly receivables are being collected. These are critical factors for any business owner to know in order to manage the business finances properly.

4. Look beyond simply profit or loss on the income statement
Of course, making a profit is your ultimate goal, but a close analysis of your income statement can reveal more than just a profit or loss. Don't just look at the numbers in isolation, but compare them from quarter to quarter or year to year to look for trends that can help you improve financial management. For example, if the operating margin (which shows how much money is being made from the basic operations of the business) is improving from year to year, this reflects an improvement in the overall operating performance of the company.

5. Use the cash flow statement to identify and understand your cash flow cycle
The cash flow statement will reveal your business' critical cash flow or operating cycle—the cycle of cash conversion from inventory to sales to receivables and back to cash again. By monitoring the cash flow cycle, you can benchmark everything from a slowdown in collection of receivables to an increase in inventory turnover.

6. Identify key financial ratios
One of the most helpful management tools you can derive from your financial statements is key financial ratios that

will help you gauge the financial health of your business. The most important small business financial ratios are:

- Current ratio—Derived from the balance sheet, this ratio shows how many times current debt could be paid off with current assets. It's used frequently by investors and lenders to measure liquidity. The formula: Current Assets ./. Current Liabilities.
- Debt-to-equity ratio—Another balance sheet ratio, this ratio measures your debt capacity. Not surprisingly, lenders are also very interested in this ratio. The formula: Total Debt ./.
- Shareholder's Equity. Accounts receivable (AR) days—This measures how long it takes you to collect the money that's owed to you. Compare your AR collection time to your terms of sale and your industry averages to see how well you're doing against your peers and your own internal standards. The formula: AR x 365 ./. Annual Sales.
- Accounts payable (AP) days—Conversely, this measures how long you take to pay your vendor invoices. You want to stretch your payables as long as possible without jeopardizing your good trade credit. The formula: AP x 365 ./.
- Cost of Goods Sold. Inventory turnover—This tells you how often your inventory "turns over" in a year. You should have specific goals for inventory turns— four times a year is a common inventory turn, but you can increase cash flow and profits without increasing sales by turning inventory faster. The formula: Cost of Goods Sold ./. Inventory

7. Recognize the potential limitations of financial statements
Most companies in the 21st century (especially self-employed individuals and micro-businesses) are based more on intellectual capital than manufacturing widgets, and their primary assets are intangibles—like ideas, concepts, branding and reputation—not equipment and hard assets. For

191

them, traditional financial statement analysis doesn't capture the full picture of the company. These companies should focus primarily on their cash flow statements.

Don Sadler, *Vice President, Editorial Director, Media 3 Publications (www.media3pub.com)—Don Sadler is a business editor and writer with 20 years of experience in the business publishing arena. Contact him at don@media3pub.com.*

10 Things Savvy Manufacturers Should Know About Crowdfunding

Crowdfunding has been a surprising way to raise funds for good causes, creative projects by musicians and artists, and product ideas from entrepreneurs. But more and more manufacturers of tangible products are finding crowdfunding a way of pre-selling new products. Crowdfunding is usually defined as using Internet-based platforms and social media to raise money through relatively small contributions by large numbers of people. This list summarizes the basic facts about crowdfunding that manufacturers should know before embarking on a crowdfunding campaign.

1. Crowdfunding campaigns raised $2.7 billion in 2012.
In 2012, the breakthrough year for crowdfunding, more than one million different campaigns raised over two billion dollars (Source: Massolution 2013 Crowdfunding Industry Report). This represented an 81% increase over 2011. All indications are that crowdfunding platforms have the potential to continue to double the amount raised each year for the next several years.

2. There are over 500 crowdfunding platforms.
New crowdfunding platforms are coming online literally weekly. And many of these are specializing in niche markets such as motion pictures, medical devices, higher education, or gaming.

3. There are at least five distinct types of crowdfunding.
Not all crowdfunding platforms are alike. One classification of campaigns identifies the variations as good cause, reward, pre-order, debt, and equity (Source: Martin Zwilling, Will

The Real Crowdfunding Model Please Stand Up). The latter three are the most relevant to manufacturers. Pre-ordering asks contributors to pay in advance to fund production of a new product. Debt-based campaigns structure a loan that will ultimately be paid back to contributors. Equity-based crowdfunding has been evolving but ultimately allows contributors to make investments in a company.

4. Crowdfunding platforms charge a fee, but they don't all charge the same amount.
Crowdfunding platforms are businesses that were started by entrepreneurs who saw an opportunity to make money. Their profit comes from fees they charge that are a percentage of the money raised. These fees can range anywhere from 2% to 10% depending on the platform. They also charge credit card fees and sometimes foreign transaction fees.

5. Most platforms make you choose between "all-or-none" and "take-what-you-make."
Some platforms only release the raised funds when the campaign hits its target amount. Others allow campaigns to take whatever amount they raise but then typically charge a higher fee.

6. It is important that potential contributors feel like they are getting a good deal.
In pre-order crowdfunding, contributors generally expect to pay less for a product than if they ordered it through other means. Manufacturers should be prepared to give a discounted price for a new product in order to be able to raise the funds in advance to produce the product.

7. Few crowdfunding platforms can attract contributors to your campaign. It's usually up to you to attract interest.
The most successful crowdfunding campaigns are the ones that can tap into a pre-existing database of potential contributors. That's why musical groups are among the most successful campaigns--they start with a "fan base" eager to see them produce a new recording. Only a few sites have the

power to attract strangers to a campaign. (Kickstarter, Indiegogo, RocketHub, RockThePost, Crowdfunder)

8. Only a few crowdfunding platforms cater to manufacturers.

Amid all the crowdfunding platforms that promote musicians, artists, non-profits, and community projects, there are some that specialize in commercial products. Crowdsupply focuses on the preordering of manufactured products and adds engineering, design, fulfillment, and warehousing assistance to the product campaigns. Unlike Kickstarter, that specifically states it is not "a store," sites such as Crowdsupply offer continued sales after even the fundraising goal has been met. Another platform, Crowdfunder, calls itself "Crowdfunding for Businesses," and adds the capability of matching manufacturers to a network of potential investors.

9. For some consumer goods, the more popular general platforms may still be your best route.

Even though they are not focused on manufactured products, some of the general platforms mentioned in #7 may be the best bet for popular consumer products. There is something to be said for being able to reach thousands of people on behalf of your product.

10. In the coming years, equity-based crowdfunding will hold the most promise for manufacturers.

The passage of the JOBS Act in April of 2012 opened up a whole new set of possibilities for crowdfunding by beginning a process of waiving a number of restrictions on publicly offering the sale of shares of stock ion a company. For manufacturers specializing in OEM and B2B products, equity-based crowdfunding provides an incentive for contributors to earn income from their contributions to successful manufacturing projects. In the coming years, this is likely to have the largest impact on the scope of crowdfunding activities.

Bob Cohen is the CEO of the Braintree Business Development Center (www.braintreepartners.org) in Mansfield, Ohio. Bob is a retired faculty member of The Ohio State University and also serves as a program coordinator for the Ohio Employee Ownership Center at Kent State University. He is a Certified Business Advisor (CBA®), a Certified Global Business Professional, and a licensed insurance agent. He is a founding board member of the Crowdfunding Professionals Association and a member of the National Crowdfunding Association. You can follow him on Twitter @doctorcohen.

7 Reasons Every Manufacturer Needs A Business Plan

If you're still not convinced that you need a business plan, then here are seven good reasons why having a business plan is a good idea:

1. Clarity in your thinking
Writing a business plan allows you to think more clearly about what you're trying to do and what you're hoping to achieve. Which in turn will make it easier to explain your idea to others.

2. Gaining a deep understanding of your target market
Taking the time out to research your business plan idea will give you a deep insight and understanding of the industry or market you're looking to enter way before you actually commit to entering it.

3. Puts the right things in the right place
A business plan pulls together all the relevant bits of information in one place such as revenue targets, expense projections, the goals for your business and the route map to get you there. Making it easier to keep track of your progress as well as keeping you focused on the long term plans for your business, all in one piece.

4. Testing out your idea
Let's be honest, many ideas sound great when you're in the pub. However, in the cold light of day when the hangover has worn off and you get it all down on paper and create your financial model, you'll discover whether it really is

possible to hit the revenue and profit targets you thought you could after a few glasses of Merlot.

5. Aligning goals

Writing a business plan is a great way to make sure that everyone is on the same page with the current and future plans for the business. If you're part of a team rather than flying solo, it's imperative that all of the team are all on the same page and agree how they'll work together on moving the business forward. If you can't agree on the where you're heading then you will probably find you won't get where you wanted to go.

6. Holds you to account

A business plan allows you to articulate your vision for your business as well as your plans to get you there. Going through the actual process of typing the words under each heading in your business plan forces you to think about creating a long term strategy for the business. Once you have answered all the questions in the business plan and laid out your timescales, it provides a simple way to track your progress and hold yourself accountable.

7. Refining your message

A business plan is a good way to describe what you do and more importantly what you do not. The very process will force you to understand who your competitors are and describe your strategy for achieving your goals. This very process will help you communicate your message to investors, employees and customers in a much more structured and effective way.

Matthew Needham consults and works with some of the world's biggest businesses, like BT, DHL and Experian as well as not-for-profit organizations such as the University of Hull and the University of Lincoln. Matthew typically consults on projects to sustainably reduce costs, improve business processes and transforming underperforming teams. Matthew can be found at bigredtomatocompany.co.uk.

10 Essential Elements Of A Manufacturing Business Plan

Every business needs a business plan – a roadmap that allows owners and management to get on the same page about how the company will achieve its objectives. In some cases, the business plan can be informal – even some scribbles on a whiteboard might be enough for some purposes. However, if the business plan will be used to raise capital from lenders or investors, it needs to be in written form – preferably no more than 20-25 pages in length. This list summarizes the essential elements of every written business plan.

1. Cover
Make sure that your cover page is neat and attractive, and be sure to include your telephone number and email. Don't make the reader hunt for this information.

2. Executive Summary
This is a brief summary of your business plan. It needs to be compelling, complete, and concise: many readers expect to get a complete picture of your business in just a few minutes, and if you don't hook them, they're lost forever. (1-3 pages)

3. Opportunity Overview
Describe the "need" in the market that you intend to satisfy. Describe the industry dynamics and where your niche falls within it. Identify key drivers and trends that affect your industry. Analyze your market to quantify current and future spending on products that meet the "need" that you have identified. (2-4 pages)

4. Products

Describe your offerings. How does it work? How does it meet the "need" you've identified? What is the "special sauce" that will appeal to buyers? What are the features? What other products are in the R&D pipeline? (2-4 pages)

5. Marketing & Sales

Identify and segment your target customers, and describe the tactics you intend to use to communicate your value proposition to them. Describe the sales channels you will use to close sales. (2-3 pages)

6. Competition & Competitive Advantages

Identify the direct and indirect competitors that serve the "need" you've identified, including substitute products. Compare the competition's strengths and weaknesses to yours. Identify the long-term competitive advantages that will help your products and your company stay ahead of the competition, including intellectual property pertaining to your product or manufacturing process. (2-3 pages)

7. Operations

Describe how your business operates, including your facilities, capital equipment, vendor relationships, supply chain, manufacturing process, logistics, inventory management, quality control, and distribution. Also, describe the principal risks facing the business and the steps you have taken to mitigate those risks. (2-4 pages)

8. Management Team

Describe the qualifications of the leadership team and key advisors. Focus on demonstrating that you collectively have what it takes to build and grow a successful company. (2-3 pages)

9. Funding & Exit

Describe the investment or loan you are seeking, and what you intend to do with the proceeds. If you are seeking an investment, describe your exit strategy – that is, how you intend to let investors cash out (typically by selling the company, or perhaps through an IPO). If you are seeking a loan, describe your plans for making scheduled loan payments (especially if the loan has a large balloon payment at the end). (1-2 pages)

10. Financial Forecast
Provide a summary 3-5 year forecast of your Income Statement, Balance Sheet, and Statement of Cash Flows. The key assumptions driving the forecast should be clearly identified and justified. The financial statements should attempt to reflect the real-world cause-and-effect dynamics that underlie your business. Describe the key drivers or metrics in your financials. (2-3 pages)

Akira Hirai, CEO of Cayenne Consulting, a leading business plan consulting firm headquartered in Orange County, Calif. For more information, please visit www.caycon.com.

Stephen Fishman, www.nolo.com. Stephen is the author of Software Development: A Legal Guide, Copyright Your Software, The Copyright Handbook, Consultant & Independent Contractor Agreements, Wage Slave No More: Law & Taxes for the Self-Employed, and Hiring Independent Contractors: The Employer's Legal Guide.

5 Key Aspects For Valuing A Manufacturing Business

Manufacturing companies are the most challenging to value given the nature of the operations and the high level of tangible assets. An appraiser who focuses on "main street" businesses – the restaurants, convenience stores and beauty salons, can easily make unintentional technical errors when performing appraisals in the manufacturing sector. The results can be disastrous for the business owner. When valuing a manufacturing business, there are five specific areas to give special attention to:

1. Excess Assets
If a company is a going concern, valuation will likely be determined using an earnings-based methodology. In its simplest form, projected earnings is divided by a capitalization rate (or multiplied by an earnings multiple) that recognizes an aggregate business risk factor. This approach provides a value for the core operational assets plus goodwill.

Often overlooked and buried within the balance sheet are excess assets that are not part of the "core" asset structure. Manufacturing companies in general are prone to having excess assets due to either inadequate management controls or the deliberate intent to avoid stock-outs. Failure to recognize these excess assets may result in a significant undervaluation of the business entity. For example, if balance sheet inventory is $1,000,000 and 10% is unrecognized excess, the business will be undervalued by $100,000. Other asset categories that need to be examined are cash, accounts receivable and machinery and equipment.

This is not a casual assessment as there are specific quantitative techniques to identify excess assets.

Unfortunately, appraisers may incorrectly assume there are no excess assets, especially if they are inexperienced in manufacturing operations. Or, they may rely on the business owner to identify excess assets even though the owner may not fully understand the concept. When separating excess assets from core assets, there are two basic questions to answer: 1) Does the asset category contribute to the revenue stream? If so, it's a core asset. 2) Is the quantity of the core asset required to contribute to the revenue stream? If not, the quantity over the required amount is an excess asset.

2. Real Estate
While most service businesses lease their facilities, many manufacturing companies operate from real estate they own. Real estate holdings can create significant complications in valuing a business, especially if the business is relatively small and generating only marginal earnings. Some of the key aspects relating to real property that warrant giving it special treatment are discussed below.

Real estate is usually a discrete asset, meaning that it can be separated from the business and deployed for different purposes. In reality, commercial real estate is a business in itself. Its current utilization may not be contributing to entity earnings at maximum potential.

The market value fluctuations of real estate may not follow the market value fluctuations of the business owning it.

Real estate does not carry the same level of business risk that is an integral factor in determining entity value.

Depreciation accounting can have a major impact on reported earning.

For small businesses in particular, real estate is likely to be a major, if not dominant, portion of total entity value.

Appraisal of real estate requires specialized skills.

Given the above factors, the inclusion of real estate in the valuation of the operational assets will almost always muddle the results. If the company owns real estate, the correct approach is to have it appraised separately by a commercial real estate appraiser. The business appraiser should assume the company leases its real estate and adjust the normalized earnings accordingly.

3. Depreciation Expense

Depreciation accounting can easily distort entity value. This is an issue for many manufacturing companies given the large amount of machinery and equipment depreciation that hits the income statement.

From a cash flow standpoint, accelerated depreciation is advantageous, but it does not properly match expense with the time period it benefits. Consider, for example, a piece of machinery having an acquisition cost of $50,000 and a useful life of twenty years. Depreciating it over its useful life results in an annual depreciation charge of $2,500. However, depreciating it over IRS guidelines results in an annual depreciation charge of $7,143 for seven years. If this period of accelerated depreciation falls into the historical time frame used for the valuation, earnings is reduced, and this in turn reduces entity value.

To avoid this distortion, depreciation expense should be appropriately adjusted at least for the high value assets. This is part of the analysis to determine normalized earnings where anomalies and discretionary expenditures are eliminated.

4. Minimum Turnkey Value

An earnings-based valuation methodology provides meaningful results only when a business is generating earnings at a level that justifies its capital investment. When a business operates at or below its economic breakeven point, an earnings-based valuation methodology returns an entity value that is less than its net asset value which is obviously illogical.

A business that satisfies the requirements of a going concern has a minimum turnkey value from the fact that it is already structured and capable of conducting business. Minimum value is based on the reality that launching a business requires a startup period to source and assemble resources, formulate operating practices, hire and train employees and establish a customer base, during which time the business operates with negative or marginal earnings. It is therefore advantageous to shrink or eliminate this startup period, and this can be accomplished by acquiring a business already operating even without earnings.

Recognition of minimum turnkey value is justified for two reasons: 1) common sense says it exists, and 2) the IRS has prevailed in tax court taking the position that it does exist. Minimum turnkey value is equal to the fair market value of net assets plus going concern goodwill and is independent of earnings. Entity value is directly proportional to earnings.
When a company is operating at point A, the derived value based on earnings is straightforward and valid. When operating at point B (negative earnings), the derived value based on earnings is negative and tells the appraiser that the valuation methodology is invalid. When operating at point C, the derived value based on earnings appears to be realistic, but is actually below minimum turnkey value.

In this case, minimum turnkey value should be used instead of the calculated earnings value. In other words, asset value overrides earnings value. If a business is only marginally profitable and the appraiser fails to recognize minimum turnkey value, it is likely that the business will be undervalued. This is one of the most common errors in business valuation. Even for a small company that is operating with only marginal profitability, the difference between minimum turnkey value and calculated earnings value can be hundreds of thousands of dollars.

5. Research and Development
Research and development is a discretionary expense that may have a major impact on calculated value. Incidental R&D can be ignored in the valuation process as it is normal for many manufacturing companies.

However, significant R&D expense needs to be adjusted from normalized earnings because it will lower the fair market value of the entity. Normalized earnings reflect only expenses that are reasonable and necessary to operate the business excluding anomalies and discretionary disbursements such as R&D. If engineering time records are not available, expenses should be allocated realistically between sustaining engineering and R&D. This breakout may have already been prepared by the tax accountant for the R&D tax credit. Also, if new products will be introduced as the result of R&D, the incremental earnings should be recognized in the projected earnings stream.

Richard P. Mager, Executive Director of Magellan Advisors, Inc., is a Certified Public Accountant and industrial engineer with over thirty years of corporate finance experience in the manufacturing sector, including twelve years of employment with Rockwell International. As an independent consultant, he provided part-time and interim CFO services to closely-held manufacturing firms. Contact him at rpmager@magellanadvisors-il.com

Chapter 6: Your Technology

5 Things Manufacturers Need To Know About 3D Printing

Also known as additive manufacturing, 3D printing is a sustainable manufacturing method that both compliments and replaces traditional, "subtractive" methods. Rather than removing material as with chipping away marble to produce a statue, 3D printing uses only the material needed, like icing a cake. 3D printing builds material up in the precise pattern desired, allowing for more complicated, functional and efficient designs with reduced waste.

1. Complexity is free

Because a 3D printer obeys the commands of your design, you can print parts or products that are as simple or complex as you like, with no added difficulty or cost. Whether your design is sophisticated or straightforward, the process for printing is simply to print.

2. Function comes first

Because complexity has no added cost, parts can be designed or reinvented for enhanced efficiency and function. Designs can revolve around the purpose of the part rather than cater to the requirements and limitations of conventional tooling methods. The incorporation of 3D printing in aerospace and automotive applications, for example, has led to reduced part count and weight, significantly improving overall performance.

3. It's fast

Also termed "rapid prototyping" or "rapid manufacturing," 3D printing is fast. Once your design is complete, you leave the work to the printer and can go from an idea to selling a product in as little as one day.

4. You have choices in technology and materials
There are dozens of systems and hundreds of materials available for 3D printing, from plastics, waxes and rubber-like materials to composite powders and metals, just to name a few. Depending on the application for which you wish to 3D print, there is almost certainly a solution in existence or development for prototyping, mold-creation or end-use parts to suit your needs.

5. It's disruptive in positive ways
3D printing allows you to print on demand, eliminating the need for expensive storage of inventory. You also have zero commitment to tooling, which means your design can continually evolve and be improved upon without significant added costs. Because designs are stored and shared digitally, it is also sustainable, with a smaller carbon footprint for global transportation. In other words: 3D printing turns the manufacturing value chain on its head.

*Article by **Jacqueline Troutman** of **3D Systems**. 3D Systems is a global, integrated solutions 3D printing company specializing in 3D printers, print materials, professional and consumer custom-parts services, and 3D imaging and customization software. 3D Systems can be found on the web at **www.3dsystems.com**.*

6 Ways Manufacturers Can Build A Profitable Digital Presence

Whether you're a smaller manufacturer who wants to get online profitably or a larger manufacturer looking to improve what you're already doing online there are principles you should follow to help you meet your goal (and avoid the situation this company found themselves in). Here are six critical ones.

1) Strategy First, Technology Second

In the movie Field of Dreams, the voice told Kevin Costner "if you build it he will come". That makes for a great movie — but that's not the way the internet works. I see too many businesses build beautiful, technologically-packed websites that no one visits because they let technology trump strategy.

2) Put Social Media in Its Place

When it comes to B2B, social media is probably the most over-hyped, time dump "marketing" method around. You would be well-served to tread very lightly with putting too many resources towards its use. And, yes, there is a time and place for social media (see the section below on becoming an object of interest). But it should likely be a small arrow in your marketing quiver.

3) Capture Contact Information

This is the most expensive mistake I see companies make online. Why? When a visitor comes to your website it's much more likely that they won't take your desired action. Often times, they're simply window shopping. That visitor then leaves, forgets about you and never returns. Most businesses have this huge "hole in their online bucket" and it's costing them a lot of money.

4) Build Relationships
In 2008 Google's CEO, Eric Schmidt, made internet waves when he proclaimed that their search engine results had become a "cesspool." What was overlooked was a comment he made at the end of his talk where he said that the companies who would do well online in the future would be those who focused on building their brand.

5) White Paper Campaigns
A well-done and strategically executed white paper campaign can be a huge boost to your digital marketing efforts and bottom line. Unfortunately, few white papers are well done or strategic. Yours can be different.

6) Object of Interest Strategy
Earlier I talked about how important building a brand and relationships will be for future success online. So now the question becomes HOW? Object of Interest Strategy (OIS). Regardless of what kind of manufacturer you are the internet gives you the technological and strategic ability that businesses have never seen before. You now have the power to disseminate your information (read: value) in as many different formats in as many different places as possible. In short, your OIS should be about "Being Everywhere."

Curtis M. Alexander is a Business Growth Strategist who helps industrial and manufacturing companies increase profits and strengthen market position. To learn more ways to grow your business request your free copy of Curtis' newest Executive Briefing: "7 Tested Strategies to Increase Profits and Lower Marketing Costs for Industrial and Manufacturing Websites" at www.curtismalexander.com.

6 Mobile Apps That Save Manufacturers Time And Money

By now virtually all businesses have discovered the value of mobile devices to their daily operations – and manufacturing is no exception. Manufacturing-related apps for smart phones and tablets continue to proliferate for iPhones, iPads, Android-based and Windows-based devices. Here are just a few manufacturing apps that have recently come to our attention.

1. Gosiger Mobile Service App, (iTunes App Store, Android Market) this custom app from Gosiger allows customers to request Gosiger's premium service 24/7 remotely, watch training videos, ask questions, take photos of their machine, keep track of machine specifications, and keep up-to-date on current news and events all from the convenience of their mobile device.

2. AutoCAD WS by Autodesk Inc. (www.autodesk.com) lets users view, edit and share AutoCAD® drawings on your mobile devices. You can open the files directly from an email and then revise, make notes, and secure approvals on the spot. Many features make it easy to use including the ability to print via HP ePrint & Share.

3. Manufacturing Material Inspection (www.qmetrixgroup.com) mobile app is available for iPhone, iPad, Android, Blackberry and Windows. It includes a barcode scanning option that enables capture of serial numbers. By entering appropriate data into the app when taking inventory or accepting material shipments, you create real-time documentation including photos.

4. Manufacturing Job Application with Tip Sheet is one of a series of apps from ComplyRight available at www.gocanvas.com. The app was created by attorneys to comply with federal hiring laws and you can get a version that also complies with your specific State regulations. It provides a list of acceptable and unacceptable questions to ask candidates and includes interviewing and screening advice.

5. Lean App, available from the Apple App Store (www.apple.com) calculates Kanbans and takes times, plus has a built-in stopwatch. The App Store also features Lean Brain Boosters, Lean Six Sigma Mobile Lite, LeanKit:Kanban and other productivity apps.

6. Mobile Repair Manager, also from the Apple App Store (www.apple.com), is designed for those companies who send service technicians into the field. It keeps track of service activities in real time so you always know the status of a repair, or maintenance order. Also provides a graphical backlog order report.

Mike Williams, Gosiger Inc.(gosiger.com) Please bear in mind that Gosiger, Inc. is not endorsing any of these apps, but simply making you aware of them. Every business has unique requirements and an app that is perfect for one company may not be right for another. The good news is that most apps are quite inexpensive and many are free, so there's not much risk in trying an app.

3 Questions To Ask Your Tech Partner

You're not a technical expert. You're bringing in an expert so that you can focus on the things you do know about. So how do you know my firm can provide a quality service? You should concentrate on these three lines of questioning.

1. Who else do you know that I know?

Start naming names: your accountant, your attorney, other people you've run into in the tech business yourself. Ask for references. See if you can find a common connection with other people in your hometown. Connect on LinkedIn and see if you share connections. Call those people and ask them about the firm. What have they heard? Any experience? Any problems? You need to get validation of the firm's services and reliability from someone you trust, or at least someone independent. If you can't find someone credible that can vouch for the IT firm then you don't want to go any further. Even in 2013 personal recommendations are the strongest validation for hiring an outside service provider.

2. Tell me about your business.

It's important to know about the firm that you're about to partner with. They will be responsible for the infrastructure that you're using to run your business. So who are you, Mr. Potential Service Provider? How many employees do you have? Do you use contractors and when? How long have youi been in business? How many clients do you have? Where would my company fall amongst your client base? Would we be one of your larger clients or smaller? Do you have any family members in your business? Where are your offices? You want to work with a business, not just some guy who's already got a full time job. Family businesses imply a livelihood and a shared goal of success. You need to see evidence of infrastructure. History. Experience. A system in place for doing business with clients. You need to be comfortable that you're not this company's first client. Or its last.

3. If I were to call you at 10PM would someone pick up the phone?

This may be extreme, but the point is this: when you have a problem will the tech provider be available to solve it? What are their support hours? Who is providing their support? If it's remote support how is that done? What is their response time? Will you have a dedicated person providing services or a support group? Do you provide mobile phone numbers and email addresses for your support people? Whatever he says...don't take his word. Test him out. Call his offices at 10PM. See who picks up the phone. Drive by his building. Stop by to say hello and see what kind of an office he runs. Ask to meet some of his support people. Are they long term employees or part of a revolving door?

Gene Marks runs a ten person technology consulting firm in Bala Cynwyd, PA. He can be reached at www.marksgroup.net

5 Ways To Make Your Manufacturing CRM System More Productive

"Our CRM software is terrible!" "Our CRM system is out of date!" "We need something that's more user-friendly." I hear this pretty frequently from my manufacturing clients. And mostly it's not true. It's an excuse.

Want to really get some value from your manufacturing customer relationship management (CRM) system? For starters, please don't have a knee jerk reaction and think that your software is the problem. Consider that you may not be the one using it very well. Bring in some experts, like your partner or vendor and have them show you all the things you're not doing with CRM that you could be doing. We'll do this for free. In particular, take a very hard look at your CRM's workflows, alerts and triggers. What are those? If you're asking, then that's your first problem. Solving this problem will significantly improve your business.

1. A workflow to handle inquiries from your website, Anytime anyone visits your website to request information, get pricing, sign up for an event or ask for a brochure you will have a workflow established so that when the visitor completes a CRM 'web-import" form, that data comes into your CRM system without duplicating the effort. The system then either creates a record for that visitor or maybe updates an existing one because you already have that visitor's email address in your system. The request is then routed to the right department/person. Emails are sent to the visitor confirming their request. Follow-up actions are scheduled so that nothing falls through the cracks. An alert is sent to a sales manager if the visitor's request is not being addressed in a timely manner.

2. A workflow to handle new leads from that trade show. You spent thousands on that trade show event in Chicago so please don't let it go to wasted. Import the spreadsheet of prospects that the trade show organizer provided into your CRM system and let a workflow that you previously designed automatically allocate those leads to your salespeople based on region or interest. Then the workflow should schedule follow-ups and tasks. Emails should be sent to those leads thanking them for stopping by your booth and to expect a call from James or Patty or whoever. Depending on their response to James' or Patty's questions the workflow could automatically add them to your quarterly mailing list or monthly newsletter. If the visitors were from an existing customer then their information is automatically added to your customer's record.

3. A workflow/alert/trigger to remind of an overdue invoice. I have a few very smart clients who have implemented alerts like this to seriously help their cash flow. The minute an invoice approaches 30 days in your accounting system a polite email is sent from their CRM system to the customer and copied to the salesperson and a next action is scheduled. After 30 days more emails are sent (professionally, of course) and the collections person, if necessary is then added to the loop. After 90 days an email is automatically sent to Tony Soprano. Just suggesting....

4. A workflow/alert/trigger about depleted inventory. Running out of inventory loses sales and annoys customers. By setting up re-order quantities in your accounting system and then configuring an alert or trigger you or your purchasing manager can be immediately aware of inventories that are running low via an email and a scheduled action in your CRM system. Taking things a step further, a well-fashioned workflow could automatically create a new order for the stock and schedule a follow--up for receiving to be on the lookout.

5. An alert/trigger or workflow to address proposals and quotas. There is nothing worse than hearing this: "Sorry boss, I forgot to follow-up on the ABC quote we sent and they went with someone else." Or "I just looked into it and ABC's sales this year are less than half what they were last year." Don't let this happen. Configure a workflow, alert or trigger to always be looking at open quotes, proposals and bids (maybe there are scheduled actions, forecasts or opportunities in CRM) and sending out reminders a week before they're coming due. And configure another one to compare the completed sales history of selected customers with a prior period and take action if volumes have fallen below a desired quota amount. One workflow I use in my CRM system is a "clients without contact" report – every month it scans my database and finds clients who have had no calls or appointments in the past six months and then sends me an automatic report. There is nothing worse than letting easy sales and happy customers fall through the cracks because you forgot about them!

Gene Marks runs a ten person consulting firm in Bala Cynwyd, PA. He can be reached at www.marksgroup.net

7 Questions To Ask Your Software Vendor Before You Buy

So you're looking for a new system. Something that will of course do the basics, like billing, payables and maintain your general ledger. But, being a manufacturer, you want much more than that. You want order entry and purchase orders. You want to manage your inventory in your warehouse. You want to track jobs as they go from stage to stage. You want detailed cost accounting that applies labor and overhead rates and calculates the gross profit on every item that leaves your shop. There are plenty of great manufacturing applications available today. You've made your list of requirements. But what should you consider before buying? What questions should you ask your software vendor? Here are seven.

1. Is your software cloud or on-premise? Software is moving steadily to the cloud. That may be good for your business. Or maybe you would prefer just to buy something outright and put it on your internal server. Or maybe you've got remote people that need access and a cloud based system makes more sense. Or maybe you don't have much of an IT infrastructure. Or maybe someday you'd like to change your mind. What cloud options are available?

2. Do you have certified partners? A good partner can make all the difference in your implementation. Having someone onsite to do the setup and training is critical for many manufacturers. Not everything can be done from the vendor's home office. Is there a partner network? Do they have certifications? Does the partner have experience?

3. How long can you test? Switching over to a new manufacturing system is a big move for many companies. So before you make the final decision it would nice to parallel for a month or two to make sure all the kinks are worked out. Does the software company allow this? What support will they provide?

4. How open is the application? What if you'd like to integrate it with other databases in your company? What if there's a great inventory management application that you'd like to purchase? Will it work with yours? How about making it talk to your website? How open is this application? Are database connectors provided? Is there a software development kit? Does the company provide development support? How many developers are familiar enough to work with the application if you'd like to really customize it?

5. Is it mobile? Can your people access purchase order information from their iPhones? Can your warehouse people make a purchase requisition from a tablet? Can your sales guys fill out an order on their laptop while sitting with the customer? Will this immediately update your system? Are there mobile apps like these available?

6. How much will this cost every year? It's not just the upfront cost, particularly if you're getting an on-premise system. But there's maintenance and support. Some manufacturers charge up to 30% of the software cost for maintenance. If you're getting a cloud based subscription then you'll have monthly costs. Is it for all users? Are there any reductions? What happens if you need more storage space?

7. What kind of support to you provide? If there's a problem at our plant in Ukraine can we call you in the middle of the night for help? What are your hours? What kind of technicians are employed in your support department? What online support do you have available? Is there an online community of other partners and customers that we can turn to? How much does support cost?

Gene Marks runs a ten person technology consulting firm in Bala Cynwyd, PA. He can be reached at www.marksgroup.net

5 IT Project Challenges For The Typical Manufacturer

We have all heard the horror stories -well intended software implementations that take too long, cost too much, or benefits never materialize. For manufacturing companies these projects typically include software installations such as ERP, supply chain management, warehouse management, manufacturing execution systems, and factory automation. While history has shown implementing large scale systems is a tough task in any industry, manufacturing companies often face unique challenges due to the type of changes involved, the nature of their business processes, and technologies used. The following list highlights some of these additional challenges or twists to the common IT project critical success factors.

1. Senior Management Commitment
Today, most practitioners understand that sr. management support and commitment to the project is critical. However, oftentimes the perceived lack of commitment is really a failure to educate management regarding what the business change truly entails and how they can effectively support the change.

The competitive pressures many manufacturers face continues to drive significant changes in operational strategies. For example, the implementation of lean manufacturing, just-in-time inventory, advanced planning systems, and even the traditional MRPII approach can require major shifts in management philosophies. In many companies, these business solutions represent not only new software tools, but also a new way of running the manufacturing operation (not just tweaking current business processes).

In the end, if senior management is not educated on the new operating concepts and practices, and the business changes necessary to achieve the benefits, they may not know how to effectively support the new system or those trying to implement it.

2. Selecting the Right Software

The software landscape is cluttered with packages that support different types of manufacturing businesses and operations. The challenge is many of the capabilities within various software packages are not necessarily unique to a specific industry and can mean different things to different people (including each software vendor).

For example, a software vendor may state their package supports companies that build-to-order, or assemble-to-order, or build-to-stock, or engineer-to-order. Furthermore, packages might be designed primarily for discrete, batch, or repetitive manufacturing processes. There are job shops, flow shops and machine shops, all with different characteristics. To make matter worse, many manufacturers require software that supports more or less all the above (mixed mode manufacturing). These complexities can make software evaluation for manufacturers more difficult and increases the likelihood of selecting the wrong package.

The key is prior to evaluating software, get educated on accepted industry definitions of these terms and thoroughly review your processes and physical work flows in the plant. Next, develop a list of software requirements and processes for the vendor to demonstrate in the software. This will allow you to more easily cut through the vendor jargon surrounding manufacturing system capabilities in order to determine if the package truly satisfies your needs.

3. The Right Project Team

Assigning the right employees from various functional areas of the business to participate on an IT project is important. Working with your IT group and software consultants, this helps to ensure the new software is designed and set up to meet the needs of the business and creates user ownership of the system.

At the same time, most manufacturing companies are fast pace environments including daily (if not hourly) production and shipping goals. Getting production out the door to meet customer expectations will always be the number priority of any manufacturer.

This creates an even tougher project staffing problem for manufacturers and the need to properly plan ahead for the resource transition. This includes defining the specific days each team member will be involved with the project. Furthermore, carefully plan and prioritize the daily responsibilities of each team member for the days they are not working in the project. Also, train other employees to back-up those involved with the project. This should start well before the project begins. Finally, plan to hire temporary or part-time employees to perform the jobs of those filling in for project team members.

4. System Integration

On most IT projects, system interfaces must be developed between the new software and current systems. The problem is the time to design, develop, and test interface programs are almost universally under-estimated. When it comes to the project costs, interface development can be a budget buster.

For manufacturing companies, not only is there a need to integrate the new system with other applications within the business, but also with a variety of hardware, software, and equipment used in the plant and the distribution center. For example, interfaces may be required to RF equipment, scanners, labelers, printers, conveyors, scales, and automated storage and retrieval systems, to name a few. This equipment likely comes from different vendors and some are developed with proprietary technologies that add to interface complexity.

Beyond properly budgeting for interfaces, the key is to minimize the scope of interface development whenever possible. First, select a software packages that provides system integration capabilities right-out-of-the box (to reduce the need for custom programming). Also, when planning the software to purchase, try to absorb as many legacy systems as possible into the new system. Finally, carefully plan the software rollout strategy to reduce the need to write temporary interfaces to legacy systems that are eventually replaced during a phased implementation.

5. Data Integrity
Within any system, certain types of business data are considered "foundational" in nature. That is, the data affects about every department using the system. Within manufacturing companies, two of the most critical data files include the bills of material and inventory records.

The bill of material (BOM) represents the raw materials, components, and assemblies required to build a particular product and the necessary quantities of each. The BOM is sometimes called the "product structure", but it is really the recipe to build the product and this information drives the entire plant.

The bills of material can be inaccurate in two forms. First, the part numbers and quantities listed in the BOM are incorrect. Second, the levels within the product structure do not depict how the product is actually manufactured or are not adequate for production scheduling purposes. Likewise, if you do not have a good grasp of the inventory of raw materials, work-in-process, and finished product in the plant, it will be difficult to run the operation effectively.

Inaccurate bills and inventory records can lead to inaccurate product costing information, quality issues, too much inventory, increased manufacturing costs, and late shipments to customers (or order cancellations). Regular audits of the BOM and inventory records are important to achieve the goal of 95% accuracy for these files.

Steve Phillips is an IT professional with over twenty-seven years of implementation experience as a software consultant and a practitioner within industry. He is the author of the book <u>Control Your ERP Destiny</u>, one of the best-selling ERP titles. His background includes senior management education, software selection, project management, application consulting, process redesign, systems design, testing, training, and post go-live support. This extensive knowledge is coupled with a rare combination of functional experience in operations management, IT management, and business reengineering. His industry experiences include manufacturing, distribution, business services, and the public sector.

Other Books By Gene Marks

In God We Trust, Everyone Else Pays Cash –
Simple Lessons From Smart Business Owners

The Small Business Book of Lists

Outsourcing for Dummies

The Small Business Desk Reference

Outfoxing The Small Business Owner

About the Editor

Gene Marks is a columnist, author, and small business owner. Gene writes daily for The New York Times and weekly for Forbes, The Huffington Post, Inc Magazine, Entrepreneur Magazine, FOX Business, and Philadelphia Magazine. His columns are read by hundreds of thousands of business managers every week. Gene has written 5 books on business management, specifically geared towards small and medium sized companies. His most recent is In God We Trust, All Others Pay Cash — Simple Lessons from Smart Business People (Create Space, 2013).

Nationally, Gene regularly appears on FOX News, MSNBC, FOX Business, Bloomberg, and CNBC discussing matters affecting the business community. Through his keynotes and breakout sessions, Gene helps business owners, executives and managers understand the political, economic and technological trends that will affect their companies so they can make profitable decisions.

Gene owns and operates the Marks Group PC, a highly successful ten-person firm that provides technology and consulting services to small and medium sized businesses. Prior to starting the Marks Group PC Gene, a Certified Public Accountant, spent nine years in the entrepreneurial services arm of the international consulting firm KPMG in Philadelphia where he was a Senior Manager.

Made in the USA
Middletown, DE
30 January 2020